CASSELL'S DIRECTORY OF

Climbers and Wall Shrubs

CASSELL'S DIRECTORY OF

Climbers and Wall Shrubs

EVERYTHING YOU NEED TO CREATE A GARDEN

RICHARD BIRD

Consultant Editor
LUCY HUNTINGTON

CASSELL&CO

Distributed in the United States of America
by Sterling Publishing Co., Inc.
387 Park Avenue South, New York, NY 10016-8810

A CIP Catalogue record for this book is
available from the British Library

ISBN 0 304 35603 4

This book was conceived, designed, and produced by
THE IVY PRESS LIMITED
The Old Candlemakers, West Street,
Lewes, East Sussex BN7 2NZ

Creative Director: PETER BRIDGEWATER
Designers: AXIS DESIGN
Editorial Director: DENNY HEMMING
Managing Editor: ANNE TOWNLEY
Illustrations: VANESSA LUFF & PETER BULL
Picture Researcher: LIZ EDDISON

Originated and printed by Hong Kong Graphic, Hong Kong

This book is typeset in Linotype Perpetua and Univers

CASSELL & CO
Wellington House, 125 Strand, London WC2R 0BB

ACKNOWLEDGMENTS

t *top* **b** *below* **l** *left* **r** *right* **Directory** *a–f, starting from top*

Liz Eddison 2, 5, 6, 10–11, 13, 14t,b, 16t,b, 19, 21, 22t, 23, 33l,r, 34l,r, 36l,r, 39r, 43, 51, 54, 66e, 87f, 95d / Agriframes 18t / Designer: Ruth Chivers, Hampton Court '99' 48 / Designer: Natural & Oriental Water Gardens 12b, 20t, 37l / Designer: Georgina Steeds 38r, 39l

The Garden Picture Library David Askham 98f / Howard Rice 91f, 101d / J.S Sira 40

John Glover 1, 4, 7, 12t, 17, 18b, 22b, 24, 28, 30–31, 32l,r, 38l, 52, 58, 60–61, 112 / David Austin Roses 26 / Designer: Julian Dowle, Chelsea 97 56 / Designer: Fiona Lawrenson 35r / Designer: Alan Titchmarsh15, 20b, 37r / Designer: Claire Whitehouse 35l

Peter McHoy 64a,b,c,d, 65d,e, 66a,b,c,d,f, 67b,d, 68a, 69a,e,f, 70d, 71e, 72a, 73a,b,c,d,e, 74a,c,d,e, 75b,d,e, 76b, 76c, 76d, 77b,d,e, 78c,d, 79a,d,e, 80e,f, 81b,e,f, 82a,b,c, 83a,c, 84a,b,c,d,e,f, 85a,b,d, 86a,b,e, 87a,b, 88b,c, 89e,f, 90a,e,f, 91a,c,d, 92e, 93b,e,f, 94a,c,d,e,f, 95b,c,e, 96a,c,d, 97a, 98a,b,c, 99c, 100d,e,f, 101a, 102c,e,f, 103b,c,d,e, 104a,f, 105a,b,c,d, 106c,d,e, 107a,c,f

The Harry Smith Collection 64e,f, 65a,b,c, 67a,c,e,f, 68b,c,d,e,f, 69b, 70b,c,e, 71a,b,f, 72b,c,d,e,f, 73f, 75c,f, 76e,f, 77a,c,f, 78b,f, 79b,c,f, 80a,c, 81a,c,d, 82d,e, 83b,d,e,f, 85c,e,f, 86c,d, 87c,d,e, 88e,f, 89a,b,c, 90b,c,d, 91b,e, 92a,b,c,f, 93a,c,d, 95a,f, 96b,e,f, 97c,d,e,f, 98d,e, 99a,b,d,e,f, 100a,b,c, 101b,c,e, 102b, 103a,f, 104b,d,e, 105e,f, 106b, 107b

David Squire 65f, 69c,d, 70a,f, 71c,d, 74f, 75a, 76a, 80b,d, 82f, 88d, 89d, 92d, 94b, 102a,d, 106a, 107d,e

CONTENTS

INTRODUCTION

Creating a garden is one of the most artistic achievements that many of us will ever accomplish. We may be hopeless with the pencil or paintbrush and yet, without ever realizing quite why, we can create something that not only gives pleasure to us, the artist, but also to everyone who visits or looks at it. A garden is a fusion of colors, shapes, and textures, which works like the best of paintings and which, like the best of paintings, has to work in three dimensions. A painting in which everything looks flat is dismissed as unlifelike and boring, and so it is with a garden. If you want to create something that you really enjoy and of which you are proud, it is essential that it works in three dimensions.

Imagine a garden that consisted of nothing but flat lawns and beds of low-growing plants. The eye would skim over it and soon be looking over the fence to see if the neighbors had produced something more interesting. Now imagine a garden full of shrubs, trellises adorned with climbers, walls, and fences smothered with flowers, and seats hidden away in fragrant bowers. There would be so much of interest going on, and there would also be an air of mystery because you would not be able to see what was happening behind every bush or behind every screen.

This is what this book is about. It is intended to stimulate the ideas that may already be half-formed in the back of your mind and spur you on to create a garden that you will be able to enjoy and in which you will be able to relax. It will build on your ideas for your garden and help you

THEN AND NOW
❧ The Hanging Gardens of Babylon was one of the earliest vertical gardens. The tiered gardens were built between 605 and 562 BC, and became one of the Seven Wonders of the World.
❧ Today, the selection of climbing and wall plants available to the gardener is wider than ever, giving everybody the opportunity to create something just as unique and special, though on a somewhat smaller scale!

enter into the third dimension so that you can make the most of all the space you have.

Vertical gardening is not only about creating a sensational picture, but about using all the available space. Many gardens are small—too small, their owners often think. Making use of walls, fences, and other vertical surfaces allows you to grow many more plants and to make a much bigger picture than if you were limited to the ground.

Stripped of their plants, gardens can be ugly places. Neighbors may peer over the boundary fences; you may have uninterrupted views of the nearby garage and sewers; the walls may be functional rather than beautiful, and the fences may have seen better days. There is no privacy and nowhere to entertain without being looked at. Once you start to consider the vertical space and fill it with plants, however, you will find that neighbors and eyesores can be excluded, while privacy and intimacy are encouraged. The

LEFT *Vertical elements screen off other parts of the garden from view, creating an aura of mystery. With containers, this can be achieved in any area. These are planted with vines.*

ABOVE *This garden mainly restricts its use of verticality to the perimeter—a traditional way of achieving privacy.*

garden becomes a much more pleasant place to be.

Apart from the enjoyment of gardening itself, most people find that relaxation and entertainment are the two most important activities made possible by a garden. Creating an environment for these is important. Shady areas are needed in which to sit or where a table and chairs can be arranged for eating and entertaining. Arbors, surrounded with scented climbers, provide somewhere for you to sit and relax, cut off from the rest of the world. Such additional features help to create an atmosphere in which our batteries can be recharged.

It is neither particularly expensive nor time-consuming to create a three-dimensional garden. You do not need a great number of plants, and you can, in any case, propagate many of them yourself from seed or from cuttings

taken from friends' plants. Using wires for supports makes the growing and training of climbing plants easy and reasonably cheap, and although trellising is more expensive, it is possible to make your own at half the cost of prebuilt panels. Even if your woodworking skills are not up to much, rustic trellising will allow you to get away with crooked joints, which will not matter as long as they are strong. Once structures such as trellises and arbors have been built they should last for years, and you should get more than your money's worth from them.

In this book we show you what a vertical garden consists of and how to achieve it. There are plenty of inspirational illustrations, as well as projects on garden features for you to follow. Finally, there are the lists of the plants that are essential for this type of garden. You will see how easy it is to transform your garden into a three-dimensional paradise. Go on, get off the ground. Reach for the sky.

HOW TO USE THIS BOOK

*C*assell's Garden Directories have been conceived and written to appeal both to gardening beginners and to confident gardeners who need advice for a specific project. Each book focuses on a particular type of garden, drawing on the experience of an established expert. The emphasis is on a practical and down-to-earth approach that takes account of the space, time, and money that you have available. The ideas and techniques in these books will help you to produce an attractive and manageable garden that you will enjoy for years to come.

Cassell's Directory of Climbers and Wall Shrubs looks at ways to add height to your garden to give it a more interesting and varied appearance. The book is divided into three sections. The opening section, *Planning Your Garden*, introduces the subject of climbing plants, looking at the different kinds of ways that you can extend your garden upward, and the range of plants that is available. There are also three specific inspirational garden plans that show suitable combinations of plants for different seasons.

Part Two of the book, *Creating Your Garden*, moves on to the nitty-gritty of selecting, buying, and planting appropriate shrubs, herbs, and flowers. Different spaces and climatic conditions, for instance, will lend themselves to different kinds of plants. This section also includes advice on the range of different garden features that you can choose from on which to grow climbing plants.

The remainder of Part Two is packed with practical information on basic techniques such as sowing, feeding, and weeding plants, supporting and pruning plants, and using containers. Moving on from this basic groundwork, this section then encourages you to put your skills to work with a series of specific projects, such as creating an arbor and making good use of trellises. There are step-by-step illustrations throughout this section that show clearly and simply what you need to do to achieve the best results. Also included are handy hints and tips, points to watch out for, and star plants that are particularly suitable for the projects that are described.

The final part of the book, *The Plant Directory*, is a comprehensive listing of over 250 plants that are ideal for adding height to your garden. Each plant is illustrated, and there is a description and a symbol chart giving complete information on appropriate growing conditions, speed of growth, and ease of maintenance. The season of interest for each plant is also given so that you can choose plants for a year-round display.

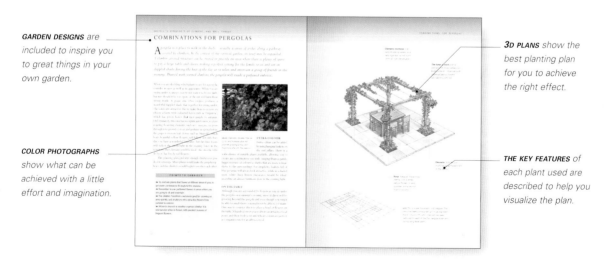

GARDEN DESIGNS *are included to inspire you to great things in your own garden.*

COLOR PHOTOGRAPHS *show what can be achieved with a little effort and imagination.*

3D PLANS *show the best planting plan for you to achieve the right effect.*

THE KEY FEATURES *of each plant used are described to help you visualize the plan.*

CHOICES show a
selection of plants,
garden furniture, or
other features that
might be appropriate
in your garden.

COLOR PHOTOGRAPHS
help you to decide
on the appropriate
feature for your
garden.

EXPLANATORY TEXT
describes the various
possibilities available
in each category.

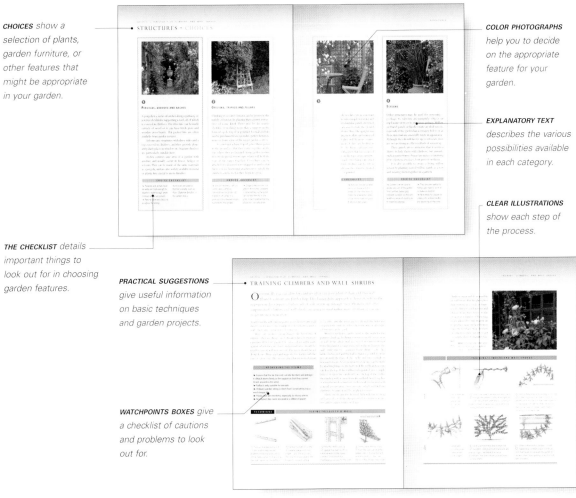

THE CHECKLIST details
important things to
look out for in choosing
garden features.

CLEAR ILLUSTRATIONS
show each step of
the process.

PRACTICAL SUGGESTIONS
give useful information
on basic techniques
and garden projects.

WATCHPOINTS BOXES give
a checklist of cautions
and problems to look
out for.

CLEAR DESCRIPTIVE TEXT
details the appearance
and the appropriate
growing conditions
for each plant.

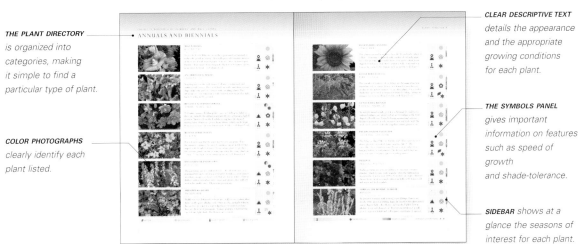

THE PLANT DIRECTORY
is organized into
categories, making
it simple to find a
particular type of plant.

THE SYMBOLS PANEL
gives important
information on features
such as speed of
growth
and shade-tolerance.

COLOR PHOTOGRAPHS
clearly identify each
plant listed.

SIDEBAR shows at a
glance the seasons of
interest for each plant.

PLANNING YOUR GARDEN

1

The idea of planning your garden may seem an onerous task to gardeners who are itching to start digging and planting, but all gardens benefit from a little bit of forethought. Rather than just charging ahead and putting in plants anywhere, spend some time considering what you are about to do—it will save hours later on, when you realize things could have been better placed, and then have to redo all your work.

LEFT *A decorative feature with a very practical purpose. With ingenuity, you can make many of a garden's inhabitants perform a dual role.*

WHAT IS A VERTICAL GARDEN?

Vertical gardening is about using all the available space in your garden: not just the flat space that the soil provides, but the whole volume of air that fills the space above it. It encourages the gardener to interact fully with the garden rather than just a part of it, while the activity of gardening becomes a much more interesting, three-dimensional experience.

Vertical gardening is a simple concept, but the rewards are great. When plants that scramble and climb upward are introduced, the whole atmosphere changes. Plants hide what lies beyond, creating an atmosphere of uncertainty and adventure, as you need to explore the garden to see all of it. The garden becomes a much more romantic place, as arbors and bowers, which are perfect for relaxation and entertaining, can be built and covered with climbing plants. Above all, there is a much greater satisfaction at what has been created, even though the work involved is not necessarily more time-consuming or arduous.

UP AND OVER

Some of the most valuable plants for the vertical gardener are those that climb up walls or over structures. These allow gardeners to exploit areas of the garden that would

REACHING FOR THE SKY

🌿 Tall plants draw the eye upward. Those with tall spikes of flowers include the biennial mulleins (*Verbascum*) and foxgloves (*Digitalis grandiflora*), hollyhocks (*Alcea rosea*), and delphinium species.

🌿 Narrow trees, shrubs, conifers and evergreen trees such as holly are useful for adding year-round structure.

otherwise not be used. At the same time they cover the boundaries of their territory, keeping out prying eyes and unwelcome noises and smells, and cover eyesores that may detract from the effect the gardener is trying to achieve.

Such climbing plants do not need to be restricted to the walls and boundaries; instead, they can be grown up structures, such as arbors, pergolas, or arches, or on free-standing poles and obelisks, whose sole purpose is to create some form of vertical emphasis. Roses, clematis, wisteria, and honeysuckles (*Lonicera*) are four such plants.

UP AGAINST IT

Not all plants that are grown against walls and fences are climbing plants. Many are what are known as wall shrubs, which are shrubs that are well suited to growing flat against a wall. For many of these, such a position is essential because they are marginally tender and the protection that the wall gives is necessary to get them through cold winters. For some, the wall offers the support they need, for they are too lanky and floppy to be of much use when grown as freestanding specimens, especially in a small garden. Others simply look good grown against a wall.

LEFT *Bamboo makes a good screening plant, but it is often better grown in a container to benefit from its oriental appeal without suffering from its tendency to invade the garden.*

VERTICAL CONTAINERS

There is no reason, however, why containers should not be attached to window sills or walls. Windowboxes, hanging baskets, mangers, and many other types of container can be fixed to walls, fences, and even to free-standing posts, so that low plants, which normally grow in beds, can be used in a vertical situation. Many of these, including pelargoniums, petunias, and morning glories, now have trailing forms, which create a cascade of bloom.

NICHE PLANTS

It is also possible to grow plants actually in a wall. This is not a good idea for house walls, but garden walls are suitable. One way is to create a niche within the wall in which a small pot or container can stand. It is best if this is put

ABOVE *Plants selected so that they do not completely obscure this attractive woven fence.*

into the wall as it is built, but it can be added later if the wall is thick enough. If not, a ledge can be created for the same effect. The other possibility, especially in older walls bonded with lime mortar, is to sow seeds of small plants into the mortar. Do not use vigorous plants, but wallflowers, aubrietia, and small wall ferns will do no damage.

NONPLANT MATERIAL

Freestanding sculptures and similar objects will add interest to the garden. Well-made and attractive garden ornaments are becoming more widely available at reasonable prices. There are also plenty of found objects that can be used, such as weathered tree stumps, pieces of iron, and items relating to gardens, such as old tools. Plaques, tiles, shells, windows, and mirrors can all be attached to walls and vertical surfaces to add further interest.

All these aspects of vertical gardening add up to an attractive style of gardening, which will transform what might otherwise be a boring patch into a space full of life and interest. It works as well, if not better, in the small garden as in the larger space.

POINTS TO CONSIDER

✿ Water can play a valuable part in a vertical garden. Fountains shoot water skyward, waterspouts spurt or dribble it out of a wall or other feature into a pool or basin, and waterfalls send it tumbling down into a pond below.

WHY HAVE A VERTICAL GARDEN?

All gardening should be about pleasure. Vertical gardening is no different in this respect. There is great enjoyment to be found in the act of creating the garden, just as there is pleasure, for both the gardener and visitors, in looking at what has been created. Simply being in attractive surroundings, in which you can relax and entertain friends, is delightful. There are also several specific, practical reasons for making vertical gardening a part of your overall design.

The first reason for making certain that you add a vertical element to the garden is for the sake of appearances. A flat garden can be boring. Break it up with vertical plantings of various types, and it will immediately become a much more interesting place.

EYESORES

Eyesores, whether they are beyond or within its boundaries, can mar enjoyment of the garden. Sometimes an eyesore can be moved or altered, but another option is to cover it with climbers. Also, ugly walls and fences may be too expensive to replace, so these too can be disguised with attractive climbers.

BELOW *Use tall evergreen plants or climbers to soften hard outlines.*

SECURITY

🍂 Boundaries are, of course, important for keeping out unwanted visitors. Plant hedges and make sure that fences are densely covered with wall shrubs or climbers, to deter people from climbing into the garden.

🍂 Impenetrable wall shrubs growing against a house help to make it difficult to gain access to windows, especially if the plant is covered with spines. Very few climbers are strong enough or sufficiently attached to the wall to allow people to climb them to gain access to upstairs windows.

🍂 Spiny shrubs include pyracantha, which tolerates sun or shade, and can be clipped to fit any wall.

FRAMING A VIEW

A garden with magnificent views may seem the ideal, but in fact, a garden may be spoiled by the views, for the eye is always traveling to them, ignoring the garden. One way of not only emphasizing the views but also the garden is to create vistas, so that the view can only be seen from certain positions, while for the rest of the time the garden itself is the focus of attention. Trellises with climbing plants, tall trees, and shrubs can all be used to create a screen that includes gaps to direct the viewer's attention.

VISUAL ILLUSIONS

A flat garden can be taken in at a glance. But when tall plants make it impossible to see everything at once, it implies that there may be more to see around the next corner. This not only makes a garden more enticing, but it also makes it seem larger. Even if a path that disappears behind a bush ends abruptly at a fence, it gives the illusion

🌸 Consider the needs of the physically challenged.
🌸 Creating a raised bed will bring the plants up to a level at which it is easier to tend to them and also to enjoy them.
🌸 Taller plants bring the flowers closer so that they can be more easily admired and, perhaps more importantly, smelled.

that it continues off some-where else. Similarly, if the boundaries are not clearly defined fences or hedges, but are disguised with shrubs and other tall plants, the garden appears to extend its actual physical limits.

ABOVE *An arch of leafy linden frames this view perfectly, creating an inviting walkway to the remainder of the garden.*

MORE SPACE

Vertical planting can be used to create more actual space, as well as the illusion of it. Although there is a tendency towards low-maintenance gardens, many people thoroughly enjoy gardening and growing plants, and they feel frustrated because their gardens are too small to grow everything they want to. By using walls, fences, and various structures, more space is made available for plants.

SHADE

One important function of a garden is to provide space in which to relax and entertain. On some days these and other activities can take place in the sun, but many people prefer a little shade, and although this can be provided by umbrellas and awnings, more pleasant shade is provided

by plants. These can be trees or tall shrubs or they can be climbers grown over a framework to create an arbor or pergola. Using plants has the added bonus that if you choose the right varieties, the shade can be scented as an extra aid to relaxation.

PRIVACY

Gardens can provide a haven from everyday life, a place where we can be ourselves and relax. Vertical gardening in the form of planting around the boundary of the garden helps to keep the outside world at bay and allow us to create our own space. No matter how friendly the neighbors may be, there are still times when privacy is all important. Hedges and climbers trained up trellises or over fences will help to block out prying eyes and, to a certain extent, sounds from a busy road.

Creating privacy is also important within the garden. Arbors can provide somewhere quiet to sit, which is not only screened from upstairs windows belonging to neighboring houses but also from other people within the same garden. They can also provide intimate rendezvous places or quiet spots for a meal. Screens make it possible to compartmentalize the garden, so that, for example, parents can sit and relax in one part while children play in another.

GARDENS-WITHIN-GARDENS

One way of making a garden more interesting is to sub-divide it into different areas—one with a country-garden atmosphere, another with a more formal planting, another for vegetables, and perhaps even one with a swimming pool. All these areas can be separated by screens or hedges, with arches leading from one to another. The trellis and archways can be wreathed in climbers. Even a small garden can be compartmentalized in this way.

CLIMBING PLANTS

*C*limbing plants are one of the basic ingredients of vertical gardening. Fortunately, such plants are neither rare nor difficult to grow. They can readily be purchased from garden centers or nurseries, and many can be grown from seed or cuttings. There are several different types of climber, categorized by means of the support they adopt in the wild: plants that are self-clinging, twining, use tendrils, or scramble.

Self-clinging climbers are plants that have developed aerial roots or suckers that cling to their support. In the wild this might be a tree, rock, or cliff face. In the garden it could also be a tree, but such climbers have a tendency to smother their supports, and so it is usually better to use them on walls or solid fences. They can climb up a wall without need for any support such as a trellis or a vine.

The main self-clinging climber is ivy, *Hedera helix*. It is best used in a wild or natural garden; in most other gardens one of the variegated or fancy forms is a better choice. The climbing hydrangea (*Hydrangea anomala* subsp. *petiolaris*) is another favorite. For autumn color the Boston ivy (*Parthenocissus tricuspidata*), the Virginia creeper (*P. quinquefolia*), and the Chinese creeper (*P. henryana*) are without parallel. All of these are very vigorous and need to be trimmed back when they reach roof level to prevent them from creeping under shingles or tiles. Unless the wall is in particularly bad condition they do no harm to it.

TWINERS

As the shoots of these plants extend, they twist around their support. In the wild the host is likely to be a tree or shrub, but in the garden it could be a pole, wire, or string support. The two most common twiners in the garden are wisterias and the honeysuckles. Both are decorative

ABOVE *Metal arches show their versatility: either freestanding or backed by a wall, they* *provide an appealing base for clematis and roses to happily ramble through.*

subjects for pillars, arbors, and pergolas. They can, of course, be grown through trees, as in the wild, but they can be rather vigorous and may eventually cover the tree. Perennial twiners, such as honeysuckle, can also constrict the growth of a tree or shrub.

In the vegetable garden, the runner bean (*Phaseolus coccineus*) is grown up strings or bamboo canes. This plant is also attractive enough to be used in the flower garden.

POINTS TO CONSIDER

❧ Annual and herbaceous perennial climbers can be grown through more vigorous climbers with bare stems at the base.
❧ Try annuals such as sweet pea (*Lathyrus odoratus*).
❧ Species of clematis that are cut back to ground level each year may be grown through other plants that have an earlier flowering season, and so do not get overwhelmed.

SELF-CLINGING CLIMBERS
- *Hedera canariensis* (Canary Island ivy); *H. helix* (common ivy)
- *Hydrangea anomala* subsp. *petiolaris* (climbing hydrangea)
- *Parthenocissus henryana* (Chinese creeper); *P. quinquefolia* (Virginia creeper); *P. tricuspida* (Boston ivy)

CLIMBERS THAT TWINE
- *Actinidia arguta* (kiwi vine); *A. deliciosa* syn. *A. chinensis*; *A. kolomikta*
- *Akebia quinata* (chocolate vine)
- *Fallopia baldschuanica* syn. *Polygonum baldschuanicum* (Russian vine)
- *Humulus lupulus* (hop)
- *Ipomoea lobata*; *I. tricolor* (morning glory)
- *Lonicera* spp. (honeysuckle)
- *Schisandra rubiflora*
- *Wisteria* spp.

CLIMBERS WITH TENDRILS
- *Campsis radicans*
- *Clematis* spp.
- *Cobaea scandens* (cup-and-saucer vine)
- *Lathyrus* spp. (peas, sweet peas)
- *Mutisia oligodon*
- *Passiflora caerulea* (passion flower)
- *Vitis* spp. (grape)

SCRAMBLERS
- *Clematis* (some)
- *Eccremocarpus scaber* (Chilean glory flower)
- *Hedera colchica* (Persian ivy)
- *Rosa* (roses)
- *Rubus* spp. (brambles)
- *Solanum jasminoides* (potato vine)

PERENNIAL AND ANNUAL CLIMBERS
- *Clematis* x *durandii*; *C. jouiniana*
- *Cobaea scandens* (cup-and-saucer vine)
- *Eccremocarpus scaber* (Chilean glory flower)
- *Humulus lupulus* 'Aureus' (golden hop)
- *Lathyrus* spp. (peas, sweet peas)
- *Phaseolus* spp. (climbing beans)
- *Rhodochiton atrosanguineus* (purple bell vine)
- *Thunbergia alata*
- *Tropaeolum majus*; *T. speciosum*; *T. tuberosum*

TENDRILS

Some climbers have modified leaves or stems that form tendrils, which wrap themselves tightly around suitable twigs. They do best when their host plant has plenty of these for them to grab hold of. Unlike clinging and twining plants, their main stems are often not in contact with a support. This can make them vulnerable in strong winds, so it is best to tie them in, especially when young, because the tendrils may not be large enough to grip properly. Once they are established, new growth will hold onto the old. They can also be trained onto wires or a trellis.

SCRAMBLERS

Many climbing plants get where they want to go simply by scrambling. They push their way up through trees and shrubs, relying on the closeness of their host's branches and twigs to keep them in place. Some have thorns or prickles, which help them stay in position as well as giving them some protection against browsing animals. Roses, of course, are the classic example of this. They will climb 20ft (6m) or more up through trees.

BELOW *Roses can be grown against walls, but will need a guiding hand to achieve exactly the effect that you want.*

WALL SHRUBS AND OTHER PLANTS

The difference between climbers and wall shrubs is rather blurred at times. This is especially true of those shrubs that can be trained to grow flat and used to cover a whole wall. Certain shrubs are also grown against walls because they are slightly tender and unable to withstand some of the lower temperatures we experience in our gardens.

Strong winds and winter wet may also cause problems for slightly tender shrubs. Walls are likely to act as "storage heaters", especially walls belonging to houses. They absorb the heat of the sun during the day and slowly release it at night—to the plants' benefit. House walls, even insulated ones, tend to leak a little of the inside warmth, adding to the plants' comfort. The protection is given to the plant as a whole, but particularly to its blossom. Fruiting plants, such as peaches and apricots, are hardy enough, but they will not fruit if their blossom is frosted. In severe winters a wall can also provide a support for a framework covered in polythene, burlap, or some other insulation material, which can be drawn over the plant.

SUPPORT AND COVER

Grown in an open garden, some shrubs have a very lax habit, forming large, open bushes, which are not only rather unattractive but also take up far too much space. When grown against a wall or a fence, however, they can be tamed. Branches can be tied in and pruned back, making a much neater plant that also flowers more prolifically.

Some wall shrubs can be grown in such a way that they cover the wall with a dense mat of foliage. They require rigorous clipping, not only to keep them in check but also to promote dense growth. The main problem with this type of habit is that it is very difficult to get behind the bush if it is necessary to do any work on the walls.

FREESTANDING TREES AND SHRUBS

Trees and shrubs can, of course, be planted in the wider garden to give height and color. Virtually any, apart from prostrate forms, can be used, but the slim, columnar forms have a greater feeling of verticality about them. Conifers, in particular, make excellent specimens. These narrow plants are particularly important in small gardens, where a wider tree or shrub would not only take up more space but would also create more shade.

ANNUAL AND HERBACEOUS PLANTS

There are many tall plants that are useful for adding height to the garden. Many have towering spires of flowers— hollyhocks (*Alcea rosea*) and delphiniums, for example, while others are simply tall and statuesque—such as the giant Scotch thistles (*Onopordum*) or the cardoon (*Cynara*). Many of the bulbs, which have slender stems, especially

LEFT Solanum crispum 'Glasnevin' (far left) forms a spreading bush with sweeping 15ft (4.5m) stems in the open, but tied back to a fence it is much more disciplined and will be covered in flowers from early summer until late autumn.

the taller alliums, create a vertical emphasis. Another series of graceful plants are the grasses, in particular the tall miscanthus and stipa.

WALL PLANTS

The range of plants that can be grown in containers attached to walls and fences is enormous. Indeed, nearly all bedding plants and many of the smaller perennials can all be grown in such a situation. The only limiting factor is that you must be prepared to water at least once a day, because such containers dry out very quickly and, because they are attached to walls, they are often protected from rain. As well as normal bedding plants, many specially adapted trailing plants are now available for hanging baskets and windowboxes.

Many of the same plants can be placed in containers held in niches or on ledges built into the wall. The plants that can grow in and on top of the wall are usually those that need a very dry situation in the wild, where they grow on rocks or scree.

BELOW *Soil tends to be drier at the foot of a wall than in other places; shrubs such as this yellow broom (*Cytisus*) thrive in well-drained soil.*

STAR PLANTS

SHRUBS TO COVER WALLS
- *Chaenomeles speciosa* (ornamental quince)
- *Euonymus fortunei*
- *Forsythia suspensa* (climbing forsythia)
- *Fremontodendron californicum* (fremontia)
- *Jasminum nudiflorum*
- *Ribes speciosum* (fuchsia-flowered currant)
- *Solanum crispum* 'Glasnevin'

EVERGREEN WALL SHRUBS
- *Azara dentata*
- *Callistemon citrinus* (crimson bottlebrush)
- *Carpenteria californica*
- *Ceanothus* 'Autumnal Blue'
- *Coronilla valentina* subsp. *glauca*
- *Cotoneaster horizontalis*
- *Desfontainia spinosa*
- *Elaeagnus* x *ebbingei*
- *Escallonia* 'Iveyi'
- *Euonymus fortunei*
- *Garrya elliptica* (silk tassel bush)
- *Itea ilicifolia*
- *Laurus nobilis* (sweet bay)
- *Magnolia grandiflora*
- *Piptanthus nepalensis* syn. *P. laburnifolius*
- *Teucrium fruticans* (shrubby germander)

WALL SHRUBS WITH BERRIES OR FRUIT
- *Cotoneaster horizontalis; C. lacteus*
- *Fatsia japonica*
- *Ficus carica* (fig)
- *Malus domestica* (apple)
- *Passiflora caerulea* (passion flower)
- *Prunus* spp. (plum, apricot, peach)
- *Pyrus communis* (pear)
- *Pyracantha* 'Teton' (firethorn)
- *Ribes* spp. (currants, gooseberries)

SPIRES OF FLOWERS
- *Alcea rosea* (hollyhocks)
- *Delphinium elatum*
- *Digitalis grandiflora*
- *Lilium regale*
- *Macleaya cordata* (plume poppy)
- *Sidalcea* 'Loveliness'
- *Verbascum bombyciferum*
- *Verbena bonariensis*

TACKLING SHADY AREAS

Some of the most difficult areas to deal with in the garden are those that are covered in shade. Gardeners who attempt to grow sun-loving plants are doomed to failure: only shade-tolerant plants should be used. Shade varies in intensity according to its position. Very few plants will grow in really dense shade, such as that found under a yew tree.

A few more plants will grow in the medium shade you find under fairly thick-canopied trees such as oaks. In dappled shade, where a shifting pattern of light penetrates, quite a lot can be grown. This type of shade is found under birch trees, for example, or those that have been pruned to allow more light through their canopy. Dappled shade is also produced by climbers, such as vines that have been allowed to grow over a pergola. Partial shade is where an area is in shade for part of the day, but in sun at other times.

IMPROVING SHADY CONDITIONS

To a certain extent, shady conditions can be improved. The canopy of a tree can be thinned out, its lower branches removed so that more light comes in from the sides. Shade cast by buildings and walls is more of a problem, but one solution is to paint the walls white so that more light is reflected onto the plants. This works particularly well if the reflecting wall is in the sun for at least some of the day.

WORKING WITH SHADE

Foliage plays an important part in planting for shady areas, because it has a much longer-lasting effect than most flowers and provides a more permanent display. It is important to use variegated and glossy foliage to brighten and enhance the interest of such areas. Yellow and silver variegations stand out in the gloom and lighten it, for instance, *Hedera helix* 'Glacier' or *Hedera colchica* 'Sulphur Heart'. Many of the shrubs with golden leaves prefer light shade. Glossy foliage, such as that of holly or camellia, reflects light and will help lift a dark spot. Plants such as the various *Parthenocissus*, including Virginia creeper, will do well on a north-facing wall, as will ivies (*Hedera*).

WATCHPOINTS

🍂 Use brightly colored foliage to illuminate dull corners.
🍂 Lighten dull areas, such as below-ground gardens, by painting the walls white to reflect the light.
🍂 Do not use sun-loving plants in shady areas in the hope that they will grow—they will languish and eventually die.

LEFT *Naturally shady gardens can often acquire a little more light through judicious pruning of overhanging trees. Increasing light levels permits a wider range of plants to be grown.*

STAR PLANTS

FLOWERING CLIMBERS FOR NORTH WALLS
- *Akebia quinata*
- *Clematis alpina*; *C.* 'Marie Boisselot'; *C.* 'Nelly Moser'; *C. vitalba*
- *Hedera* spp. (ivy)
- *Hydrangea anomala* subsp. *petiolaris* (climbing hydrangea)
- *Lonicera* spp. (honeysuckle)
- *Parthenocissus* spp.
- *Rosa* 'Albéric Barbier'
- *Rosa* 'New Dawn'
- *Rosa* 'Veilchenblau'
- *Schizophragma hydrangeoides*

SHRUBS FOR SHADE AND NORTH WALLS
- *Camellia japonica*
- *Chaenomeles speciosa*
- *Choisya ternata*
- *Cotoneaster lacteus*
- *Crinodendron hookerianum*
- *Desfontainia spinosa*
- *Euonymus fortunei*
- *x Fatshedera lizei*
- *Fatsia japonica*
- *Garrya elliptica* (silk tassel bush)
- *Ilex aquifolium* 'Angustifolia'
- *Jasminum nudiflorum* (winter jasmine)
- *Pyracantha* 'Teton'

CLIMBERS FOR SHADE

In the wild, many climbers—roses, clematis, and honeysuckle, for example—start off in shade but then scramble up through the trees until they reach the sun. Although they can grow in shade, they only flower properly in the sun. In a garden, shade cast by a relatively low wall or shrub does not cause a problem and the climber will flower where it can be seen. In the shade of a tall building, however, flowers are likely to appear well out of sight.

A few roses will flower in shade, and *Rosa* 'New Dawn' is the prime example of a plant that is happy on a north-facing wall. *Clematis* 'Nelly Moser' also prefers this position to full sunlight, when the petals are prone to bleaching. Honeysuckles also enjoy light shade, but their roots must be kept moist or the plants will not perform well.

WALL SHRUBS FOR SHADE

Fortunately, a number of shrubs will tolerate the open shade of a north wall. *Garrya elliptica*, with its long silver tassels, is doubly welcome because it flowers in winter. Winter jasmine (*Jasminum nudiflorum*), the ornamental quince (*Chaenomeles*), and camellias are other examples of shrubs with this double virtue.

Euonymus fortunei is a very good foliage plant because it will grow not only against north walls but also in quite deep shade. The variegated forms are particularly useful and really illuminate shady areas.

BELOW Clematis *'Nelly Moser' is particularly suitable for a shady garden, as the flowers fade in strong sunlight.*

WARM, SUNNY GARDENS

Warm, sunny positions in the garden are among the easiest areas to cope with, as there are so many plants from which to choose. Indeed, in many respects the gardener is spoiled for choice, and one major advantage and attraction of growing plants in sunny conditions is that it encourages many to give off a fragrance, something that colder conditions inhibit.

On the whole, all climbers can be grown in a sunny garden without any serious problems. Needless to say, however, as with all aspects of gardening, there can be difficulties, and in this instance the main concern will be dry conditions. While most shrubs are perfectly happy in the sun as long as they have plenty of moisture around their roots, many will not do as well when the ground is dry.

CLIMBERS IN SUNNY POSITIONS

In the wild most climbers use trees or shrubs for support, and as a result many of those that we grow in our gardens have a preference for "cold toes and hot heads". In other words, their roots like cool shade, but the flowering stems should be in full sun. Clematis plants, in particular, demand these conditions. Fortunately, it is not difficult to provide this environment in the garden, where it is a simple matter to cover any root areas that are in full sun with mulch, a few tiles, or pieces of stone. In many cases, of course, the roots of plants such as clematis are shielded from the effects of the sun by other plants in the border around them and there is no need for extra action.

The other problem facing the gardener who wishes to grow climbers against walls and in sunny positions is that the soil is likely to be dry. Most climbers, including clematis and honeysuckle, prefer moist soil. Honeysuckle, for example, becomes much more prone to aphid attack and to the production of sticky honeydew if it is allowed to get too dry, and many varieties of clematis suffer if the soil becomes dry for lengthy periods. Adding plenty of well-rotted organic material to the soil and ensuring that you water thoroughly during prolonged dry periods will overcome these problems.

SHRUBS IN SUNNY POSITIONS

A wide range of shrubs will grow in sunny positions, and the gardener should have no problem in finding enough for such a situation. Some shrubs that normally grow in full sun have golden-leaved forms, and these need to be given some shade, especially from the hot midday sun, to prevent the leaves from scorching.

As with climbers, some shrubs may suffer from too little moisture in the soil. This is particularly true of those planted near a wall, where the soil has a natural tendency to be much drier than that in the rest of the garden.

One other problem is that a sunny position is, by necessity, an open one, and this may mean that the area is exposed to winds. If these are strong they may physically damage the shrubs by breaking limbs or even the whole plant, and also cause wind scorch on the leaves. Some form of windbreak will be needed in such conditions.

LEFT *Roses, hollyhocks, and other tall flowers create intriguing, colorful "walls" along this sunny path, interspersed with lower-growing lavender and campanula.*

🌺 South walls can be very warm, which can be a problem in summer for plants that prefer cooler or shadier conditions.
🌺 In winter, south walls can be used for marginally tender plants that appreciate the protective warmth.
🌺 Soil at the foot of south-facing walls can become very dry, so keep plants well watered.

LEFT *A jumble of plants of different heights brings a bed to life—here a color-themed blend of foxgloves (which also like shade) and allium.*

ANNUALS AND PERENNIALS IN THE SUN

All the annuals and perennials with a vertical emphasis are sun lovers and present no problem under such conditions. The only possible problem is that when such plants are grown against a wall or fence, even a sunny one, they tend to lean forward, partly from a desire to get even more light and partly because of the draft caused by wind being bounced off the wall behind them. Staking or tying to a wall support will overcome this.

PLANTING AT THE BASE OF DRY SUNNY WALLS

The area in front of a wall, especially a south-facing wall, is often very hot and dry. This can make it very difficult to grow normal garden plants there and there is every reason to make a virtue out of necessity and create a Mediterranean garden or border. These may not be as exotic as they sound, but they are a way of exploiting a difficult condition to your advantage.

STAR PLANTS

🌺 *Clematis* 'Ernest Markham'
🌺 *Itea ilicifolia*
🌺 *Jasminum officinale*
🌺 *Lathyrus odoratus*
🌺 *Lonicera periclymenum* 'Serotina'
🌺 *Rosa* 'Bantry Bay'

The basic idea is to use plants from the various places around the world that have a Mediterranean climate, plus those from more temperate areas that like similar conditions. Shrubs such as the rock rose (*Cistus*) are ideal. These offer attractive flowers and many of them have a wonderful resinous smell. The flowers only last a day, but there are always plenty more buds for the next day. *Buddleja*, *Cytisus*, *Genista*, *Hebe*, all good drought-resisting shrubs, can be used to give the bed height as well as color. Silver-foliaged shrubs such as *Convolvulus cneorum* and the daisy bushes, *Olearia*, do particularly well in these conditions.

There are a number of tall annual and perennial plants that will add to the height of these beds. Since the moisture is often a long way down, it is mainly the taprooted plants such as the mulleins (*Verbascum*) and sea hollies (*Eryngium*) that are ideal plants. Bulbs with tall slender stems, such as the alliums, also love these conditions.

There are not many climbers that can be used, but bougainvillea can be overwintered in a conservatory or warm greenhouse and brought out in its container to be used in such a bed, or simply placed against a warm wall. A few more tender climbers that are usually confined to the conservatory can also be used in the same way. Roses and the jasmines will often grow in these dry circumstances, especially if they can get their roots well down to where the moisture lies.

The bed can be covered with small stones or gravel to give it the right ambience. A more imaginative solution would be to landscape the gravel and bed to make it look like a dried-up river bed.

GARDENING IN WINTER AND SPRING

It may be cold and wet outside, but nature is awake and there is always something happening in the garden, and there are more than enough climbers and wall shrubs to make an attractive display at this time of the year.

It is possible to get carried away and to cover the house walls with plants that will look good together at just one time of year, overlooking the fact that there are another eleven months to get through. You should aim to have a mixture of shrubs and climbers that will provide interest throughout the year. It is sometimes possible to plant a late-flowering climber so that it grows through something that finishes blooming much earlier in the year. For example, the winter-flowering silk tassel bush (*Garrya elliptica*) is rather dull for most of the year, but it can be cheered up by planting one of the summer-flowering viticella clematis to grow up through it.

CLIMBERS

Very few climbers produce flowers in winter. The main exception is, surprisingly perhaps, a clematis, *C. cirrhosa*, which is most commonly grown in its form *balearica* or 'Freckles'. It has small, bell-shaped flowers, which are cream in the species and cream spotted with red in its various forms. In spring several clematis come into

BELOW *Wisteria's glorious spring display is shown to full effect on a pergola, making a fragrant walkway to stroll under.*

flower. *Clematis montana* is widely grown, and it is a good climbing plant with white or pink flowers and a wonderful vanilla scent. Wisteria puts on its magnificent floral display in late spring, although it may take several years to reach its full potential.

SHRUBS

Winter jasmine (*Jasminum nudiflorum*) has bright yellow flowers that stand out against the vivid green stems. It does not grow tall and is suitable for growing under a window. Flowering quince (*Chaenomeles*) is another shrub that can flower in winter and, like the jasmine, it has a long season, blooming from late autumn into spring. It should be kept cut back tight to a wall or a fence. The flowers are in shades of red and pink.

Camellias should be planted where they do not catch the early morning sun, which can damage frosted flowers before they have been able to thaw out. As noted above, garryas are good for winter interest, although they are not colorful plants because the tassels of flowers are silver. The scented azara, however, produces color in spring when its haze of yellow flowers open.

WINDOWBOXES

Windowboxes can be filled with winter pansies to give color throughout winter and spring, and an underplanting of daffodils will brighten up the end of winter and hail the coming of spring.

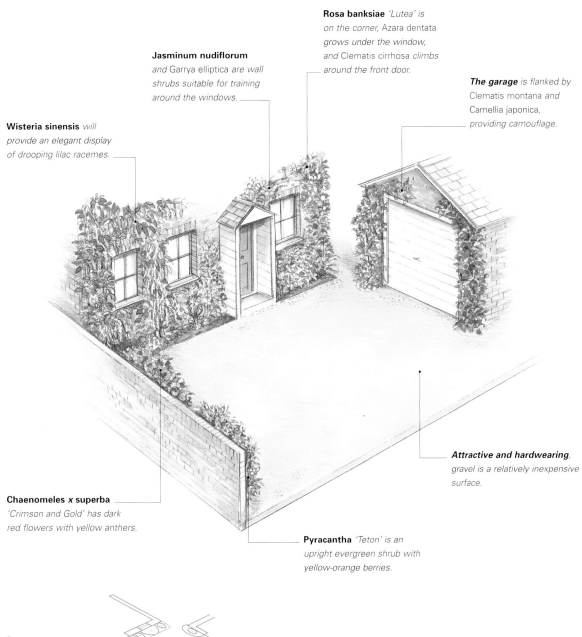

Rosa banksiae *'Lutea' is on the corner,* Azara dentata *grows under the window, and* Clematis cirrhosa *climbs around the front door.*

Jasminum nudiflorum *and* Garrya elliptica *are wall shrubs suitable for training around the windows.*

The garage *is flanked by* Clematis montana *and* Camellia japonica, *providing camouflage.*

Wisteria sinensis *will provide an elegant display of drooping lilac racemes.*

Chaenomeles *x* superba *'Crimson and Gold' has dark red flowers with yellow anthers.*

Pyracantha *'Teton' is an upright evergreen shrub with yellow-orange berries.*

Attractive and hardwearing, *gravel is a relatively inexpensive surface.*

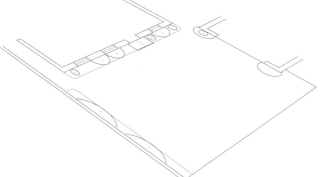

LEFT *This is a plan for the area immediately outside the front door of the house. The garage determines that most of the area is covered in gravel as a turning and parking space. The house faces south, so receives a lot of sun.*

GARDENING IN SUMMER AND AUTUMN

There is so much going on in the garden in summer that it is tempting to wonder if there is a need to add to the display. As we have already noted, however, vertical gardening is important and should be well represented at this time of year just as much as at others. Indeed, this is the time when climbers are at their best, with roses, honeysuckles, clematis, and many more in flower. Gardeners who have planned ahead will have left gaps between winter climbers and wall shrubs for plants that have things to offer at other times of the year.

These may be filled with plants that flower in summer or have some other virtue, such as attractive berries, in autumn. There is also the opportunity to grow some climbers through shrubs and other climbers that have flowered early in the year. *Clematis cirrhosa* tends to look rather bare around its base, but planting a summer-flowering *Eccremocarpus scaber* would cover the lower stems of the clematis and brighten them up. The viticella clematis are also excellent for growing through other plants. They are cut back almost to the ground each winter, so the host flourishes unimpeded before the viticella takes over when it is past its yearly best.

BELOW *Nothing beats the sensual perfume of roses. Grow over a pergola or arbor for maximum enjoyment.*

POINTS TO CONSIDER

🍃 Try to keep a balance of plants coming into flower throughout the summer and into the autumn.
🍃 Some plant varieties have a long flowering season, or a second flush of flowers, and these should be used in preference to those with shorter seasons.
🍃 If possible, include some scented plants, as warm walls are just the place to bring out their perfume.

CLIMBERS

As the wisteria and clematis of spring fade, roses take over. There are so many from which to choose that narrowing the choice may be difficult. Many of the older varieties have the advantage that they are scented, but the disadvantage that they flower over a relatively short season. Modern varieties often have a main flowering followed by a gap and a repeat flowering, or they continue to produce a few blooms throughout summer, but not all modern roses are fragrant. Try to go for something like *Rosa* 'New Dawn', which has beautiful pearly pink flowers that continue nonstop for months, and also has a delightful fragrance.

Summer is also the time for annuals like sweet peas (*Lathyrus odoratus*). Again, perfume is the dominant factor—or it should be, because many modern strains are scentless. Grow sweet peas up pyramids or through low shrubs.

Once autumn comes and the end of the growing season approaches it is the autumn foliage that catches the attention. The striking colors of the Virginia creeper (*Parthenocissus quinquefolia*) and Boston ivy (*P. tricuspidata*) can scarcely be bettered. Fruit also plays an important role at this time of year, so a pyracantha with red or yellow berries is an attractive addition.

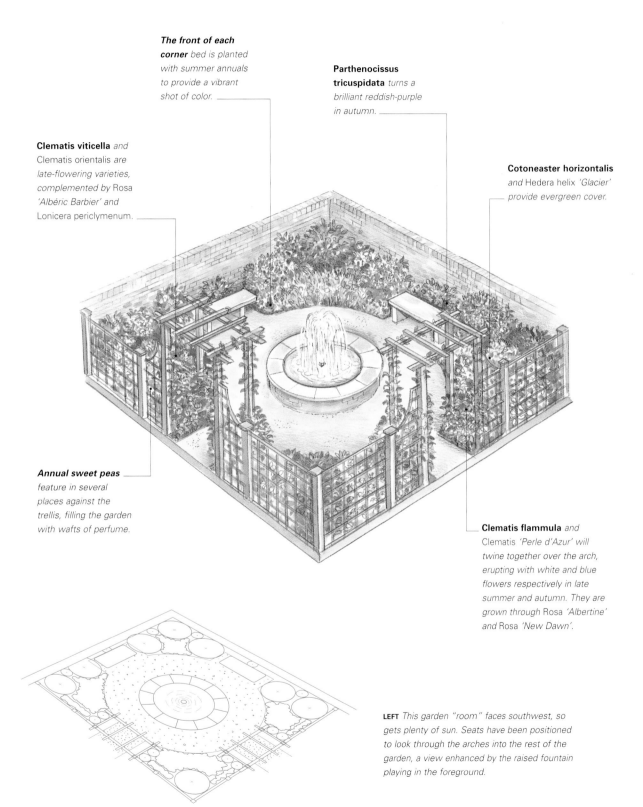

The front of each corner *bed is planted with summer annuals to provide a vibrant shot of color.*

Parthenocissus tricuspidata *turns a brilliant reddish-purple in autumn.*

Clematis viticella *and* Clematis orientalis *are late-flowering varieties, complemented by* Rosa *'Albéric Barbier' and* Lonicera periclymenum.

Cotoneaster horizontalis *and* Hedera helix *'Glacier' provide evergreen cover.*

Annual sweet peas *feature in several places against the trellis, filling the garden with wafts of perfume.*

Clematis flammula *and* Clematis *'Perle d'Azur' will twine together over the arch, erupting with white and blue flowers respectively in late summer and autumn. They are grown through* Rosa *'Albertine' and* Rosa *'New Dawn'.*

LEFT *This garden "room" faces southwest, so gets plenty of sun. Seats have been positioned to look through the arches into the rest of the garden, a view enhanced by the raised fountain playing in the foreground.*

COMBINATIONS FOR PERGOLAS

A pergola is a place to walk in the shade—usually a series of arches along a pathway, covered by climbers. In the context of the vertical garden, its form may be expanded. A climber-covered structure can be created to provide an area where there is plenty of space to put a large table and chairs, making a perfect setting for the family to sit and eat in dappled shade during the heat of the day, or to relax and entertain a group of friends in the evening. Planted with scented climbers, the pergola will exude a perfumed embrace.

When you are deciding which plants to use for a pergola, consider its uses as well as its appearance. When you are sitting under a canopy, you do not want it to be too dark, but nor should it be too open, or the sun will burn those sitting inside. A grape vine (*Vitis vinifera*) produces a wonderful dappled shade that is perfect for sitting under. The leaves are attractive, but to make them even more so choose a form with colored leaves such as 'Purpurea', which has green leaves that turn purple in autumn. Unfortunately, this vine has no significant flowers, so plant a spring-flowering clematis, such as *C. montana*, to grow through it to provide color and perfume in spring before the grape is even in leaf. A rose such as 'Maigold', which bears beautiful yellow flowers, will follow; not only does this rose have a wonderful fragrance, but the shiny leaves will reflect the candlelight in the evening. Later in the season another clematis would be ideal—*C.* 'Ville de Lyon' has lovely red flowers.

This planting plan provides enough climbers to give decent coverage. More plants would make the pergola top-heavy and the climbers would begin to smother each other.

ABOVE Clematis *'Ville de Lyon'* and honeysuckle will provide glowing color and fragrance late into the season.

EXTRA COLOR

Extra color can be added by using hanging baskets on the end pillars. There is a wide choice of suitable plants available, allowing you to create any combination you wish, ranging from a garish, happy mixture of colors to shades that are more sympathetic to the surroundings. For simplicity, baskets full of blue petunias will always look attractive, while in a shaded spot, white busy Lizzies (*Impatiens*) would be ideal, providing an almost luminous glow in the evening light.

ON THE TABLE

Although you are surrounded by flowers as you sit under the pergola on a summer's evening, most of these will be growing beyond the pergola and even though you might be able to smell them, you might not be able to see many. One way to counter this is to place a bowl of flowers on the table. A bunch of sweet peas is always an attractive focal point, and their fresh scent and delicate color are perfect accompaniments for an alfresco meal.

POINTS TO CONSIDER

🍂 Try and mix plants that flower at different times of year, to get some variety throughout the seasons.

🍂 Remember to use perfumed flowers in areas where you are going to sit and entertain.

🍂 The climber *Passiflora caerulea* is good for covering an area quickly, and produces very attractive and fragrant flowers from summer to autumn.

🍂 *Wisteria sinensis* is another vigorous climber. It is spectacular when in flower, with pendent racemes of fragrant flowers.

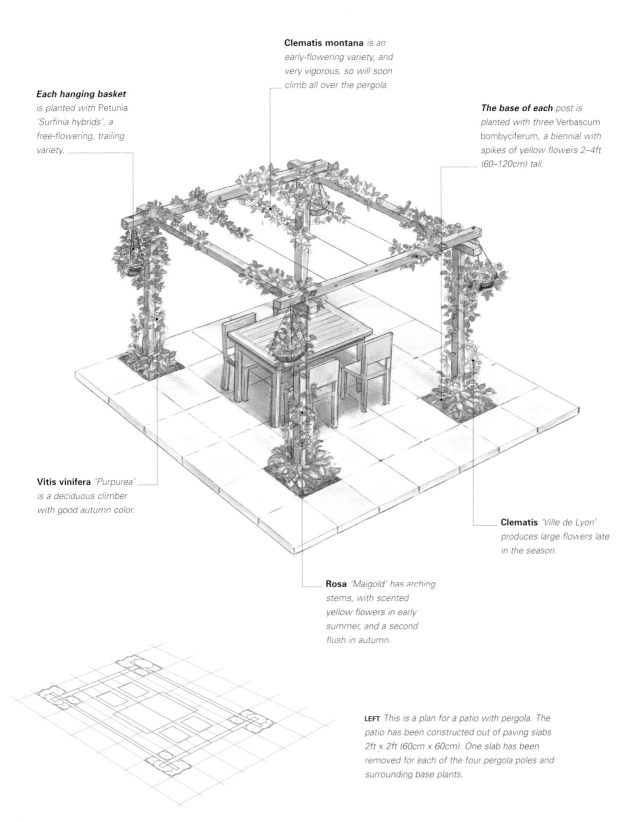

Clematis montana *is an early-flowering variety, and very vigorous, so will soon climb all over the pergola.*

Each hanging basket *is planted with* Petunia *'Surfinia hybrids', a free-flowering, trailing variety.*

The base of each *post is planted with three* Verbascum bombyciferum, *a biennial with spikes of yellow flowers 2–4ft (60–120cm) tall.*

Vitis vinifera *'Purpurea' is a deciduous climber with good autumn color.*

Clematis *'Ville de Lyon' produces large flowers late in the season.*

Rosa *'Maigold' has arching stems, with scented yellow flowers in early summer, and a second flush in autumn.*

LEFT *This is a plan for a patio with pergola. The patio has been constructed out of paving slabs 2ft x 2ft (60cm x 60cm). One slab has been removed for each of the four pergola poles and surrounding base plants.*

CREATING YOUR GARDEN

2

Various elements, besides plants, make up the vertical garden. For example, you may erect a structure such as a pergola, or install other vertical features such as a fountain with a vertical spray of water. Incorporating just one of these features into even the smallest garden will increase the garden's interest and appeal.

LEFT *Successful gardening comes down to working with nature, not against it. If an area does not get much light, you must plant shade-tolerant plants such as this elegant white-flowered deciduous climber,* Hydrangea anomala *subsp.* petiolaris.

STRUCTURES · CHOICES

PERGOLAS, ARBORS, AND ARCHES

A pergola is a series of arches along a pathway, or a series of columns supporting a roof, all of which are covered in climbers. The structure can be made entirely of wood or it can have brick piers and wooden crossbeams. Kits are often available from garden centers.

Arbors are structures with three sides and a top covered in climbers, and they provide pleasantly shady places in which to sit. Fragrant climbers are particularly suitable here.

Arches connect one area of a garden with another, and usually occur in fences, hedges, or screens. They can be made of the same materials as a pergola, and are also widely available in metal or plastic kits (metal is more durable).

CHOICE CHECKLIST

❧ Pergolas and arches must be wide and high enough for people to walk through when climbers are in full growth.

❧ Place a table and chairs in an arbor for dining.

❧ If roses are used, a thornless variety, such as *Rosa* 'Zéphirine Drouhin', is the safest choice.

OBELISKS, TRIPODS, AND PILLARS

Climbing roses and clematis can be grown in the middle of borders by planting them against a structure of some kind. These may be decorative obelisks, or nothing more than a support in the form of a pole tripod or pyramid. Formal obelisks can be purchased from specialty garden furniture companies or from some of the larger garden centers.

To construct a basic tripod, place three poles in the ground so that they come together at the top, where they are fastened. Some garden centers now stock special tripod caps, which will hold the tops of the poles together. Crossbars can be attached or galvanized wire wrapped around so that there is some horizontal attachment to which the climbers can be tied as they begin to grow.

CHOICE CHECKLIST

❧ Annual climbers, such as sweet peas (*Lathyrus odoratus*), can be grown up wigwams of bamboo canes or a pyramid of brushwood simply pushed into the ground.

❧ Single poles can also be used in the border, wrapped in wire netting, or the plant can be tied directly to the pole. Once it reaches the top, allow it to cascade down.

TRELLIS

Trellis can be as simple or elaborate as you want it to be. Basic trellis provides simple screening and consists of square or rectangular panels stretched between posts. These are inserted into the ground to a depth of at least 24in (60cm). The uprights can be supported by nothing more than earth rammed around the base, but they will be more secure, especially in windy areas, if they are set in concrete *(see pages 58–59)*. More elaborate trellising can be created with panels that have a curved upper edge and finials on the tops of the uprights. Archways can also be made of trellising. Like other woodwork in the garden, trellises can be left as natural wood, in which case they must be treated with wood preserver, or painted.

CHOICE CHECKLIST

❧ There is little point in buying the more elaborate trellis styles and patterns if they cannot be seen, so do not cover this type completely with climbers.

❧ Natural-colored wooden trellis will blend with the plants. On the other hand, to make the ornamental nature of the trellis stand out, paint it white or dark green.

SCREENS

Other structures may be used for screening— perhaps to obscure an unsightly object or unpleasant view, or to give more privacy. Willow, cedar, and hazel panels or hurdles make an ideal screen, especially if the garden has a cottagey feel to it, as these materials are essentially rustic in appearance. Although they should last for up to ten years, they are not as strong as other methods of screening.

These panels are so attractive that it seems a shame to hide them with climbers, but annuals, such as nasturtiums (*Tropaeolum majus*) or morning glory (*Ipomoea tricolor*), look perfect on them.

It is also possible to create a living willow screen by planting rooted willow whips in a row and weaving them together in a pattern.

CHOICE CHECKLIST

❧ Screens can be used to divide one part of the garden from another. Leave gaps between screens, as this will lead to a sense of mystery as to what lies beyond.

❧ They are very useful for hiding ugly objects, such as oil tanks or garbage cans.
❧ New ideas for shapes to create with willow hurdles are appearing all the time.

ORNAMENTS • CHOICES

STATUES AND SCULPTURES

Statues and other forms of sculpture have been used outdoors since the first gardens were laid out, and they have a relationship with plants that somehow seems perfect, the living plants complementing the inanimate object and vice versa.

Sculpture can be set in a formal position to mark the end of a path or in some other prominent site to draw the eye toward it. More informally, it may be positioned so that a visitor to the garden comes across it almost by accident.

Most sculpture looks much better when it is set on a plinth. Such a base should be solidly constructed; a wobbly heap of loose bricks is dangerous and likely to cause a serious accident if it is surmounted with a heavy statue.

CHOICE CHECKLIST

ও Create focal points or arouse interest with items such as old tools and gardening equipment.
ও Try garden centers for affordable sculpture.

ও Interesting branches and chunks of wood, even weather-worn pieces, can be used to enhance planting designs. These "sculptures" do not have to cost money.

WALL MASKS

It is not always possible to grow plants up walls, but it is usually possible to fix various objects to the wall to break up the flat surface and to create points of interest. A wide range of objects can be used, but one of the most popular are ceramic masks. These are available in several forms and styles, but the ones most often seen and most widely available are tiles with masks embossed on them. The tiles can be cemented to the wall, or, if you prefer something less permanent, they can be held in position with mirror clips. Instead of masks, many other decorative objects are suitable for hanging on the wall—even a piece of weather-worn wood can look very attractive. Old tools can also be wall-mounted.

CHOICE CHECKLIST

ও Brush the wall to remove loose material, before using waterproof tile adhesive.
ও Avoid getting adhesive on the wall around the mask—keep it directly under the tile.

ও Use shiny objects in dark corners so that they add sparkle and life to what might otherwise be a rather dull area.

MIRRORS

Mirrors can be useful, especially in a small garden. Set on a wall and perhaps surrounded by a creeper so that the edges cannot be seen, they will appear to be windows or doorways offering a glimpse into another part of the garden. What will be seen, of course, is a reflection of the real garden.

Mirrors can also be used to reflect light into dull areas. This is particularly handy in below-ground gardens, where they will throw light into gloomy corners so that more plants can be grown.

A third use of mirrors is to use small ones and broken pieces as part of a mosaic, which will add glitter and shine to the garden and brighten up the wall where it hangs. Small mirrors can also be hung so that they sparkle as they turn in the wind.

CHOICE CHECKLIST

❧ Take great care with mirrors if young children use your garden.
❧ By cleverly positioning mirrors, you can make the garden seem larger.

❧ Disguise the edges of the mirror with a climber and place one or two potted shrubs or other plants in front, to add to the depth of the illusion.

PAINTED WALLS AND MURALS

The most straightforward approach is to use a single color, and white is a good choice if you want to reflect light into a dark corner. Exterior wall paint gives a long-lasting, durable finish, but the range of colors is not huge. Emulsion paint is not designed for exterior use, but it is cheap and cheerful and easy to apply. The drawback is that you will have to redo it every so often, although a weathered look often enhances its appearance.

A skillfully executed mural can be a visual illusion, with doors, gates, or windows apparently opening out into other, as yet unseen and unexplored parts of the garden. Such a *trompe l'oeil* can make it seem as if a modestly sized garden is just a tiny corner of a vast estate.

CHOICE CHECKLIST

❧ Consider the impact that painting your walls will have: do not opt for an effect that will conflict with the garden as a whole, or one that you are likely to tire of.

❧ Trellis on painted walls should be hinged at the base, with a clip at the top (see page 42). This allows the trellis to be eased away so that the wall can be painted.

WATER FEATURES* • CHOICES

❶ FOUNTAINS

A fountain creates a wonderfully variable verticality as the column of water rises, drawing the eye upward with it. Several heads can be fitted to the pump, to create effects ranging from a single column to several columns in a variety of patterns. You need not restrict the fountain to a single jet from one source, however, and if you have the space several different sources within or around the same pool would create an eye-catching display. The pump can shoot the water up from below the source of the pond or it could be part of a sculptural feature that is mounted above water level.

A fountain is an ideal focal point, especially in a formal planting, but a simple feature in an informal garden would be equally effective.

CHOICE CHECKLIST

- ❧ The spray from a fountain should not blow over surrounding paving.
- ❧ Incorporate lights below the fountain if you plan evening entertaining nearby.

- ❧ Never take risks with electricity and water, and get a qualified electrician to install pumps and lights. Follow the safety instructions for using the equipment.

❷ WATER SPOUTS

Spouts fitted to a wall or pillar will send a single arching stream of water down into a small pool or into a reservoir hidden beneath a layer of large pebbles or stones. The most basic spout could simply be a short length of pipe appearing out of the wall, but there are many more interesting designs available, including the traditional face—often a lion's face or Neptune's—with the water emerging from the mouth.

To give height to your water feature, there is no reason why you should not install several spouts, which could all play into the same point in the pool in a symmetrical arrangement, or which could all point at different angles, creating a confusion of arching streams of water.

CHOICE CHECKLIST

- ❧ If there are children around, water spouts are safer than an open pool.
- ❧ Trickling water spouts hardly take up any room and are ideal for small gardens.

- ❧ Water spouts allow you to use your ingenuity and imagination, and lend themselves to all sorts of designs.

* Always build in a drainage system, especially in colder climates where freezing is a problem.

WATERFALLS AND CASCADES

A sheet of water has quite a different visual and emotional impact to a fountain. It may pour over the top of a wall, arching forcefully into a pool. If preferred, the flow could be reduced to little more than a trickle so that it actually runs down the wall, bubbling out and around any defect in the surface. Or use a large-capacity pump to build a really lively cascade, in which water tumbles over rocks.

When you are building any structures that will contain water it is crucial that the top is absolutely horizontal or the water will not flow evenly. It is also important to choose an appropriate site within the garden; avoid positioning the feature so that water runs down a house wall or through a fence or hedge into a neighbor's garden.

CHOICE CHECKLIST

❧ Waterfalls incorporated in streams are only really suitable for larger gardens. However, you can create a fall of water from a height, then pump it up again.

❧ Only build waterfalls and cascades if you like the sound of running water. Most people find it restful, but some are irritated by it.

SURPRISE, SURPRISE

Long before electronics made such things easy, fountains were devised that switched themselves on as people walked passed, just to amaze them. A column of water suddenly shooting up beside you can certainly be surprising. In some cases the fountains were disguised as very naturalistic trees, which suddenly spouted water.

Electronic eyes to switch on the pumps are now relatively cheap and easy to install, making the control of surprise fountains much easier. However, do remember that electricity and water do not mix and can be very dangerous unless you know what you are doing. Employ a qualified electrician to help if you are in any doubt. The electrician may also have some ideas to contribute.

CHOICE CHECKLIST

❧ Do not aim the surprise fountain directly at the victims or they might get soaked—unless you are really wicked!

❧ A magic eye can be used to switch the water on when there is somebody in the garden, preventing waste of water and electricity.

PLANTING IN AND ON WALLS • CHOICES

PLANTING IN WALLS

There are several ways of planting in walls. Plants or seed can be pushed into crevices in drystone walls or into the soft mortar joints of old walls. Walls can be built with a recess along the top, which can be filled with soil and planted. When you are planting in walls, it is important that there are drainage holes so that excess water can drain away.

You might find that it is easier to sow seed than to insert plants into a narrow crevice. Place the seed on the palm of one hand and hold your hand against the wall. Then use a drinking straw to blow the seed into the crack. Drought-loving plants, such as wallflowers, do best in these conditions, although walltops can be decorated with a variety of other plants.

CHOICE CHECKLIST

∾ Walls can be built specifically to enclose a raised bed. These have traditionally been used mainly for alpines, but could be filled with any plant.

∾ Do not overplant the vertical surfaces of a wall. A few choice plants look best.
∾ Most flowering plants prefer to be on the sunny side of the wall.

WINDOWBOXES

Windowboxes can be placed on windowsills or hung on the wall, either immediately below windows or elsewhere on walls, fences, or even posts. They are made in a variety of materials, from terra-cotta, which can be heavy, especially when filled with soil, to lightweight plastic, or you can make your own from wood. As with hanging baskets, there is a very wide range of plants available, either to grow yourself from seed or to buy as plants from garden centers.

Always make sure that windowboxes are securely attached *(see pages 48–49)*. You will have to water at least once a day, so make sure they are easy to reach and do not make it impossible for you to open your windows.

CHOICE CHECKLIST

∾ Bright flowers, such as pelargoniums, always look good against walls, especially in sunny positions.
∾ In shady areas, go for *Impatiens* or foliage plants.

∾ Even with water-retaining crystals added to the soil, windowboxes will still need watering most days, unless there has been heavy rain.

HANGING BASKETS AND CONTAINERS

One of the easiest ways of adding color to walls, posts, or even trees is with hanging baskets. There is an enormous range of colorful plants that can be used to fill the baskets, many of them being common garden plants that have been bred to trail rather than stand upright. Try a cheerful mixture: it seems that you can get away with violent color clashes in a hanging basket that you would not dare introduce into your beds or borders!

A vast array of other hanging containers can be used too. Proper planters, usually ceramic, are available from garden centers, but homemade containers work just as well—even shiny tin cans can be pressed into use. Make sure that all containers have drainage holes in the bottom.

CONTAINERS FOR CLIMBERS

Climbers tend to be vigorous plants, so use a large container made of a durable material, because the climber is likely to be growing in it for many years. Plastic and cheaper terra-cotta pots may shatter. A heavy-duty container will provide some root protection in winter; in very cold weather add a layer of extra insulation around the outside, such as straw, burlap, or even plastic bubble-wrap.

Fill planting containers with a good-quality potting soil. Water-retentive crystals can be added to help prevent the soil from drying out too quickly, but it is still likely that you will have to water the containers once a day. You should apply a liquid feed once every two weeks during the growing season.

CHOICE CHECKLIST

- Check that hanging basket brackets are secure.
- Do not position baskets to overhang where people walk.
- Do not put tender plants out until after the last frost.
- Hang baskets at a convenient height for watering.
- Containers make eye-catching features when hung from a tree or post.

CHOICE CHECKLIST

- Put containers in position before filling with soil, as they can become very heavy.
- For perennial climbers, replace the top layer of soil each year.
- Cover the soil with stones to prevent the sun overheating the plant's roots.
- Water daily and feed every 14 days during the growing season.

PROPAGATING YOUR STOCK

Half the battle in growing climbers and shrubs, or any other plants for that matter, is to ensure that you acquire good plants in the first place, that the ground is thoroughly prepared, and, after planting, the plants are well nurtured until they are established. If this is done then the foundations are set for healthy, floriferous plants.

One of the most crucial tasks in gardening is the thorough preparation of the ground that you are going to plant. It must be absolutely clear of perennial weeds. Annual weeds can be pulled out as they appear, but perennials can be very difficult to get rid of, especially if they have run through the roots of a climber or shrub. Delay planting until the spring, when any perennial weed that has been left in the soil should have shown itself and so can be removed.

Dig deeply not only where the plant is to go but also, bearing in mind that the roots will spread out widely, in the area around. Incorporate as much well-rotted organic material as you can. Garden soil, farmyard manure, leaf-mold, composted bark (but not chipped bark) will all do. This humus will provide a slow release of nutrients to the soil and hence the plant, and it will also hold moisture without becoming waterlogged.

SEED

Collecting seeds from the garden allows you to produce a large number of plants at very little cost. However, plants grown from seed are not always true to their parents. Seed from a white rose, for example, might produce a pink or red rose that only grows to half the parent's height. So if you require a plant that resembles its parent, use cuttings.

BUYING PLANTS

Always look for healthy plants, and reject any that are sickly, covered with pests, or look drawn and leggy. They do not necessarily have to be the biggest of the bunch— medium-sized ones are likely to

LEFT *Most roses can be propagated from hardwood cuttings in early autumn.*

TECHNIQUE   **HARDWOOD CUTTINGS**

1 In winter make a slit in the ground with a spade. If the soil is heavy, open it further and trickle some sharp sand into it.

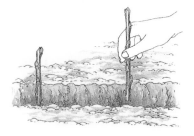

2 Insert the cuttings, which should be about 6in (15cm) long, so that about half is below ground.

3 With your feet, tamp down the soil around the cutting, closing the slit. Transplant cuttings when they have rooted.

HINTS AND TIPS

❧ The two basic methods for propagating climbers and wall plants are growing them from seed or taking cuttings. A propagator (a structure that provides a humid atmosphere) is useful, but many gardeners manage perfectly well by placing pots of seed or cuttings into a polythene bag to provide the required atmosphere.

❧ Semi-ripe cuttings can be taken from most shrubby plants during midsummer. These are placed in a cutting soil and kept in a warm and moist atmosphere until they have rooted. Hardwood cuttings are taken from the dormant climber or shrub in winter and placed in a slit in the ground in a shady place in the garden where they will not be disturbed. The slit is closed and the cuttings left until they have rooted, when they can be dug up and transplanted or moved into pots. Roses are a good subject for this method.

TECHNIQUE — SEMIRIPE CUTTINGS

1 Remove the top 4in (8cm) of a non flowering shoot. Cut the stem cleanly just beneath a leaf and then take off all the leaves except for the top two. Cut the stem of clematis above a pair of leaves.

2 Fill a 3in (7cm) pot with potting soil. Dip the bottom of the cutting into a rooting powder. Make a hole in the soil near the rim of the pot and firm in the cutting. Several cuttings can be put in the same pot.

3 Water the pot and then place it in a polythene bag, ensuring that the bag does not touch the leaves of the cuttings. Place in a warm, light position out of direct sunlight.

4 When the cuttings have rooted, lift them gently, taking care not to harm the roots, and pot them up into individual pots.

settle in faster and grow more quickly. Choose climbers with a good structure of strong shoots. A good shape is more important than size. If possible, check that the plant is not pot-bound (a mass of roots wound around and around inside the pot). Such plants are often difficult to establish, the roots being reluctant to set off into the surrounding soil. Inspect the roots by turning the pot on one side and gently sliding the root ball out.

TECHNIQUE — SEEDS

1 Fill a pot with a good-quality sterile sowing soil. Press it down very lightly with the base of another pot and then scatter the seed thinly on the surface. (The picture shows clematis seed.)

2 Cover the seeds with a layer of fine grit or a thin layer of soil and water. Do not forget to add a label. Place in a polythene bag and put in a warm spot out of direct sunlight.

3 When the seedlings have germinated and have their second pair of leaves, they are ready to prick out. Remove each seedling from the pot, holding it by its leaves. Plant in an individual pot.

TRAINING CLIMBERS AND WALL SHRUBS

*O*ccasionally you can abandon climbers after you have planted them and they will flourish without any further help. This laissez-faire approach is, however, only really appropriate for rampant climbers, which will swarm up through trees. On walls and other supports both climbers and wall shrubs are going to need more attention if you are to get the best from them.

Apart from the self-clinging plants, most climbers and wall shrubs need some form of support to hold them against a wall. There are several ways of doing this.

Wires are, in most circumstances, the best form of support. They are cheap, easy to fix, and relatively discreet, especially if they are painted the same color as the walls against which they are fixed. Galvanized wire should be used because it will not corrode. The wires should be set about 18in (45cm) apart and supported by traditional vine eyes or screw eyes. The eyes are placed at intervals of about 4ft (1.2m), and the wires are fed through the holes and secured at the ends. In order to keep the wires really tight, a tensioner can be used.

Wooden trellising can be fixed to the walls for the plants to climb up. Trellising is best restricted to small areas of wall. If the whole wall is covered, it tends to detract from the plant it is supporting. Screw the trellising to the wall and use spacers—wooden blocks about 1in (2.5cm) wide—between it and the wall so that it is possible to wrap ties around the bars of the trellis and easy to tuck in wayward shoots. A less permanent structure can be made by attaching hinges to the bottom of the trellis and a secure catch to the top. If the wall has to be painted, it is a simple matter to open the catch and ease the top of the trellis, the climber with it, away from the wall and then to replace it when the work is finished. Trellis should be treated with a wood preservative (not creosote, which will kill the climbers) because it will be in place for years.

Plastic mesh can also be used. Although this is cheap and easy to attach with the clips provided, it is not very attractive and becomes brittle with age.

ATTACHING THE STEMS

🌺 Ensure that the tie does not cut into the stem and damage it. Attach stems firmly to the support so that they cannot thrash around in the wind.
🌺 Raffia is only suitable for annuals.
🌺 Ordinary garden string is short-lived; tarred string has a much longer life.
🌺 Plastic ties are excellent, especially for thorny plants.
🌺 Avoid plant ties (wire encased in a ribbon of paper).

TECHNIQUE — FIXING A TRELLIS TO A WALL

1 Attach two wooden battens to the wall in the planned position of the top and bottom of the trellis panel. Drill and plug the wall; screw on the battens.

2 Fasten the bottom of the panel in place with two hinges: 1–3in (2.5–7.5cm). Thoroughly oil and grease the hinges to prevent rusting.

3 Fold the trellis back up against the wall and attach a catch at each of the upper corners. Undo these for maintenance access to the wall.

4 For access to the wall, gently ease the top of the trellis away. Do not force it back too quickly or the main stems of the climber may break.

TRAINING

Fan the young shoots of climbers out as widely as possible at the base of the wall. This will ensure that the plant gives a good coverage rather than growing as a single column. Arch over the shoots of woody climbers, such as roses and solanum, in a semicircle before fixing them firmly to the support. This will promote a greater number of flowering shoots and buds. If stems are allowed to run straight up the wall they are likely to produce most of their flowers at the top of the wall, leaving the rest bare. Stop climbers before they get to the roof, otherwise they may try to get beneath the shingles or slates and loosen them. Remember to keep both climbers and shrubs clear of windows and doorways.

RIGHT *Climbing roses need good air circulation if grown against walls, to prevent mildew.*

| TECHNIQUE | TRAINING CLIMBERS AND WALL SHRUBS |

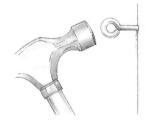

1 Insert conventional vine eyes at intervals of 4ft (1.2m), with about 18in (45cm) between each row. Traditional eyes are hammered into the wall, but it may be necessary to drill a pilot hole first.

2 Attach the wire to an end eye and pull it through the others. Pulling it as tight as you can, secure the other end by twisting it back on itself. If necessary use a tensioner (a long bolt with an eye in it).

3 Train arching shoots by pulling down one of the long stems so that it forms a graceful arch and tie it to the wire supports. Do the same with all the other shoots so that it looks like a fountain, with stems shooting out on each side.

4 Plastic ties are the most convenient method of attaching stems to the wires. Wrap it round both stem and wire, insert the end through the hole, and pull it tight.

5 Each year tie in the shoots that will inevitably spring up from those already tied in. Again, tie these in a curve. Eventually, the wall will be covered with arching stems.

6 When either tied-in climbers or self-supporting climbers reach roof level, trim them back to beneath the gutter to prevent them from getting under the roof shingles or slates.

PRUNING

Pruning is one aspect of plant care that many gardeners try to ignore, hoping that it will go away. With most trees and many freestanding shrubs, you can get away with taking no action, but most plants benefit from attention, and once a gardener has tackled pruning a couple of times, it becomes as routine as many other garden activities and no longer a job to be dreaded and put off.

The appropriate time to prune varies from plant to plant. As a rule, the best time for pruning those plants that flower on old wood is soon after the climber or shrub has finished flowering. This gives the plant a chance to produce new shoots, which will be nearly a year old by the next flowering season. Plants that flower on new wood should be pruned in spring so that a new crop of shoots is produced ready to flower in the same year.

BASIC PRUNING

Pruning has several functions, the first of which is to remove any dead or dying wood. Cut any such wood right back to the base or to where it joins wood that is still growing. Next remove any damaged wood—that is, any stems and branches that have been broken or on which the bark has rubbed off through contact with another branch. Diseased wood should also be removed. The next task is to remove weak wood—that is, growth that is thin and drawn. You should also take out branches that will not be of any benefit to the plant. Cut these back to sound wood.

Climbers and shrubs on walls, arches, or pergolas must be kept back tight to the structure, or wayward stems may catch passersby. Many of the stems that stick out can be tied in, but, particularly with shrubs, it may be difficult to persuade these to lie flat. Cut the unruly stems back to a fork within the bush or climber instead.

HINTS AND TIPS

❧ Once a wisteria has covered its allotted space it must be kept tightly under control if it is to flower well, and this is normally achieved by pruning twice a year. After flowering, cut back any new growth to about 6in (15cm) of the old growth. In winter reduce these shoots further to about 3–4in (8–10cm), cutting just above the second or third bud.

TECHNIQUE   **PRUNING CLEMATIS**

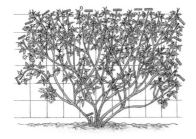

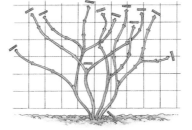

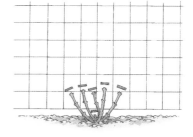

1 Group 1 are early-flowering clematis and the species with small flowers, such as *C. montana*. No pruning is required except the removal of dead wood. They can be cut back after flowering if they are outgrowing their allotted space.

2 Group 2 are large-flowered cultivars that flower on the previous season's wood. First remove all dead material and then cut back all other stems to the first pair of strong buds from the tip of the stem. This should be done in late winter.

3 Group 3 are those clematis that flower on new wood, including all the small viticella cultivars. After the dead growth has been removed, cut all stems back to a sound pair of buds about 2ft (60cm) above the ground. Do this in late winter.

Branches of shrubs grown against a wall may cross each other. When these are tied in so that they cannot move, there should be no problem. However, branches of free-standing shrubs or trees that travel across or through the bulk of the others may cause damage and should be removed. Even in a wall shrub, such crossing of branches can cause congestion, and a few may have to be removed for the sake of the others.

Many wall shrubs need to be kept cut back tight to the wall, and it is important to cut the new season's growth back to within two or three buds of the old wood. The old wood can easily be identified by its darker color and harder bark. One or two shrubs, such as holly (*Ilex*), can be treated almost like a hedge and trimmed back with shears to keep them in a neat shape.

To keep climbers and shrubs vigorous and healthy, it is important to encourage new growth. The way to do this is to remove a certain amount of the old wood to stimulate the growth of new wood from the base. The rule with most climbers and shrubs (but not trees) is to remove up to a third of the oldest wood each year. This could, however, be excessive in some cases and may, for example, make any display a bit thin. In such cases simply remove what you can without ruining the overall shape.

There is a handful of shrubs that merely need all the stems to be cut to buds just above the ground each year in late winter, such as most buddlejas, some elders (*Sambucus*), and the viticella group of clematis. Other shrubs require specialized pruning, notably certain varieties of clematis and wisteria.

TECHNIQUE **BASIC PRUNING**

1 The thinner pieces of wood that are cut with pruning shears should be pruned with a cut that starts just above a bud and slopes back at 45 degrees toward the main stem.

2 Do not cut too far away from a bud, causing the long piece of stem above the bud to form a "snag" that dies back, sometimes taking the rest of the stem with it. Also avoid cutting too close to a bud.

3 When removing larger wood with a saw, make a first cut in the underside of the branch, 6–9in (15–23cm) from where you intend to cut off the branch. This cut should go about a quarter of the way through.

4 Make another cut about 1in (2.5cm) further out along the branch, this time cutting right through the branch.

5 Move to your final position and cut straight through the branch. The idea of the first two cuts is to remove the weight of the branch and prevent it from splitting, taking part of the trunk with it.

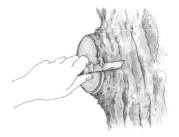

6 Cut away any rough edges around the cut but do not paint the wound, which used to be recommended.

CARE AND MAINTENANCE

Care and attention lavished on climbers and shrubs will repay the gardener, who will have healthier, more floriferous plants. Plant maintenance may seem daunting to the beginner, but it is not difficult or time-consuming. If you perform the simple jobs regularly it will seem less of an overwhelming chore.

Weeding is the pet hate of many gardeners, but when all perennial weeds are removed from the start, you stand a much better chance of keeping control. It is best to weed during winter if at all possible. Warm weather is a time of rapid growth for weeds as well as other plants!

TECHNIQUE	WEEDING

1 It is safer to weed by hand. Hoes can be used but can accidentally damage plants. Remember to remove the roots of the weeds as well as the visible part.

2 Once a bed has been weeded, cover with a mulch—well-rotted organic material, such as manure or garden compost, or composted bark chippings are ideal. Apply a layer up to 4in (10cm) deep.

TECHNIQUE	WATERING

1 To water a hanging basket, tie a hose to a bamboo cane. Various attachments are also available to facilitate watering.

2 If the soil becomes very dry, stand the basket in a bowl of water until bubbles cease to rise from the soil.

DEADHEADING

Unless a plant has attractive fruit heads, there is no doubt that a climber or shrub that is regularly deadheaded looks much more attractive than one that is not. Deadheading can be a chore, especially if, for example, you have a rose that covers the whole of one side of the house. If you feel the effort is worth it, go ahead; if you do not, do not worry.

WATERING

It is essential that newly planted shrubs and climbers are watered until they are established. Aim to provide weekly at least the equivalent of 1in (2.5cm) over the whole root area. Mulching with organic material will help to prevent evaporation from the surface of the soil.

FEEDING

Every spring and autumn top-dress the soil around the plant with well-rotted organic material. This will not only act as a mulch but also supply nutrients to the soil, like leafmold in the wild. If you have no organic material available, in early spring apply a top-dressing of a general fertilizer at the rate specified on the container.

TECHNIQUE	FEEDING AND SPRAYING

1 Feed container plants every 10–14 days in the summer, using a fertilizer dissolved in water. Water the soil first.

2 Inspect plants regularly for pests. Spray with an environmentally friendly pesticide if required.

STAKING AND SUPPORTS

Inspect climber supports and stakes for shrubs and trees regularly. Make sure that they are still sound and not coming away from the wall or ground. Check that the plants are still secured to them and tie in any wayward shoots (particularly important with roses, because thorny stems can cause injury). Check the ties on trees and make sure that they are not digging into the trunk. Most are adjustable and can be slackened off when necessary.

Also check arbors, pergolas, arches, and trellises, especially wooden ones. When covered with climbers these structures create an enormous resistance to the wind, and if they are not in good condition they may blow over. They are then extremely difficult to reerect.

Rot round the base of wooden supports is one of the main causes of weakness. It is sensible to apply a preservative to all wooden supports on a regular basis, but do not use creosote, which will kill the plants.

TECHNIQUE	VERTICAL STAKE

1 Dig out the planting hole and then pound in the stake. Position the stake on the windward side of the tree, with the top just below the lowest branch. Spread out the tree's roots, cover with soil, and firm it.

2 Then, secure the trunk to the stake in at least two places. About six months later, recheck the "ties" to ensure that they are secure but not strangling the trunk.

TECHNIQUE	OBLIQUE AND H-STAKE

1 Using this method, the stake is inserted after the tree has been planted. It is an ideal staking method if a tree has to be restaked after the original one breaks. The stake's top must face the prevailing wind.

2 This type of stake is inserted after a tree has been planted and often as a remedial method if a tree's first stake should fail. It is also suitable where a tree has a large root ball

TECHNIQUE	SUPPORTING HERBACEOUS PERENNIALS

1 Insert three strong stakes around a plant and encircle them with strong green string.

2 Manufactured metal stakes inserted around a plant help to support weak stems. They are ideal for supporting peonies.

3 Twiggy sticks are the traditional way to support herbaceous plants. Insert them early in the year, so that stems and leaves grow up and through them.

CONTAINER SHRUBS

❧ The attention given to climbers and shrubs growing in containers differs from that given to plants growing in the ground only in that they need more watering and feeding. Except in wet conditions and unless they are very large, most containers need watering at least once a day. This constant watering quickly leaches (washes away) nutrients from the soil, and these should be replaced by adding a liquid feed to the watering every two weeks or by inserting a stick of slow-release fertilizer into the pot.

USING CONTAINERS

In smaller gardens, especially those that are completely paved, containers may be the only way of growing climbing and wall plants. However, containers are useful in any garden. Windowboxes and hanging baskets will brighten up walls, fences, or other places that can support them. With careful planning, they can be kept filled all year round.

When they are full of soil, containers can be extremely heavy, especially as those used for climbers or wall shrubs are likely to be quite large. It is sensible to place them in their final positions before filling them.

Two of the most important aspects of growing plants in containers seem to be contradictory: the container must be free draining, yet at the same time the soil must be moisture retentive. This apparently incompatible advice means that excess water should be able to drain away, as few plants like to sit in stagnant water, but the soil must also retain sufficient moisture for the plant's use.

FILLING AND PLANTING
Drainage is vital, and the bases of all containers should have drainage holes in them. When you are planting in a container, add a layer, 1–3in (2.5–8cm) deep, of broken pottery or small stones in the bottom to help excess water drain away. Fill the container up to the top with a good-quality potting soil and gently firm down.

If you wish, you can make two additions to the soil before you fill the container. The first of these is water-retaining crystals, which absorb excess moisture and slowly release it when the roots want it, thus reducing the amount of watering required. The other is slow-release fertilizer granules, which will do away with the need for subsequent feeding for the year. Follow the directions on the containers for quantities and use.

Make holes and set the plants in the containers so that the tops of their root balls are level with the surface of the soil. You may have to add more soil to bring it to the right height. Firm in the plants and water thoroughly.

MAINTENANCE
Climbers and wall shrubs are too large to repot, so the best you can do is to remove some of the soil from the top and replace it with fresh materials every spring, but take care that you do not disturb the roots. The slow-release fertilizer will have been used up, so add some more to the new soil. You can also insert a fertilizer stick or plug into the container, which will slowly release nutrients into the soil in the coming growing season. Feeding is not necessary if you use a slow-release fertilizer. If you do not, use a liquid feed every two weeks.

Unfortunately, unless they are very large, containers dry out quickly and will need watering every day and even more frequently in hot, dry weather. Do not rely on rainfall because the containers, which will be against a wall and sheltered by the shrub or climber, may not get as much water as you think.

WINDOWBOXES
Colorful pelargoniums, trailing petunias, delicate bulbs, and others will make a vibrant scene outside the window. Keep boxes well watered, and make sure you cut back straggly stems and fading flowers.

LEFT *Using dramatic color contrasts focuses lots of attention on this pergola.*

PROJECT | **WINDOWBOXES**

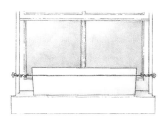

1 All windowboxes should be firmly fixed in position to prevent them falling. One way to secure a box is to strap it in place with a length of strong galvanized wire. Attach it to screw eyes screwed into holes (drilled and filled with plugs) in the wall.

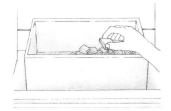

2 To ensure good drainage, place a layer of crocks (broken pottery) or small, irregular-shaped stones in the bottom of the box. The layer should be about 1in (2.5cm) deep. Make sure that they do not block the drainage holes.

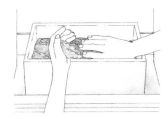

3 Fill the windowbox with good-quality potting soil. You can mix water-retaining crystals and slow-release fertilizer granules with it before filling the box if you wish. Gently firm down the soil. Do not fill the box to the brim.

4 Make holes in the soil with your hand or a trowel and place the plants in the holes. The tops of the root balls should be level with the surface of the soil in the windowbox. Firm down the soil around the plants.

5 Smooth over the surface of the windowbox, ensuring that the surface level is at least 1in (2cm) below the rim of the box. If you have not added fertilizer granules, press a slow-release stick into the soil. Water thoroughly.

6 Water the box every day; on very hot days with a drying wind this will need to be done twice. Add a liquid feed to the water once a week. Remove all dead flowers and cut back any wayward stems that look a bit straggly.

PROJECT | **HANGING BASKETS**

1 A hanging basket bracket must be securely attached to the wall, fence, or post. Drill and plug the holes, and screw the bracket on.

2 Place the empty basket on a bucket while you work. Put the liner in place and fill it with a good-quality basket soil. Lightly firm it down.

3 To insert plants in the side, wrap the roots in wet tissue and pass through a hole cut in the liner. Remove the tissue. Add soil in stages.

4 Baskets above head height can be suspended on a pulley system and lowered for watering. Or use a long, curved breaker head to water the baskets.

TOPIARY

opiary can play an important part in a garden. Although, in reality topiarized plants are little more than shrubs, the fact that they have been "sculpted" creates quite a different image from a free-growing bush. The control exercised over the plant seems to epitomize the control over nature that is, essentially, what gardening is all about. There is something about the neatness of the clipped surfaces that appeals to most of us. Slow-growing trees or shrubs with a compact structure are the most suitable.

Box (*Buxus sempervirens*) and yew (*Taxus baccata*) are tight and compact. Box and yew are undoubtedly the best plants to use, especially if you want to make complicated or well-defined shapes, but holly (*Ilex*) will also hold its shape well and will tolerate being clipped. If you want to create simple blocks there are plenty of other plants to choose from, including euonymus, privet (*Ligustrum*), and some conifers. Sweet bay (*Laurus nobilis*) provides rounded shapes.

EXISTING SHRUBS

There are two ways to create topiary. The first method is simple and easily accomplished: take an existing shrub and cut it to shape. You will have to choose a shrub that regenerates, such as yew or holly, and the main problem is that the plant will look unattractive until all the bare patches have grown over, which may take a couple of years. This approach will be appropriate only for simple shapes, such as boxes or obelisks.

GROWING FROM SCRATCH

A much more satisfactory, although slower, method is to grow the topiary from a small shrub, training it in the direction you want it to grow, and pruning out extra branches.

Trim the branches as they reach their ultimate position. Thus, if you want to make a ball and if the plant is already tall enough, trim off the top and any side branches that extend far enough. Using a hoop of stout wire as a gauge and holding it over the bush in several positions, clip back any branch that touches it. Eventually the shrub will have filled out enough for the ball to be complete.

SIMPLE SHAPES

Most simple shapes—boxes, cones, balls, and pyramids, for example—are self-supporting. Nevertheless, it can still be a good idea to make a former (a device to put inside to hold the shape), not so much for support but to act as a cutting guide to keep the shape regular.

PROJECT	BOX PYRAMID

 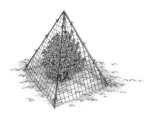  

1 Prepare the ground thoroughly, adding plenty of well-rotted organic material. Plant a young box (*Buxus sempervirens*) shrub so that the root ball is level with the surface of the surrounding soil.

2 Construct a framework out of four metal rods pushed into the ground and four pieces of rigid wire netting. Make sure that the shape is upright and regular, and that the plant is in the middle of it.

3 As the shrub grows, the branches will stick through the mesh. Clip them back to within 1in (2.5cm) of the wire netting.

4 Eventually, the box will cover and hide the wire and the supporting framework, which can be used as a guide to keep the pyramid in shape. Trim back once or twice a year to within 1in (2.5cm) of the framework.

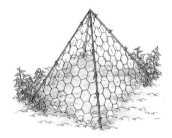

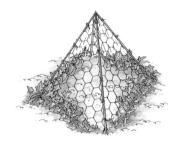

1 Make up a framework as for the box (*Buxus*) (*see previous page*) and plant two ivies (*Hedera*) at opposite corners.

2 Tie in the stems, spreading them out so that they go around the base of the whole pyramid.

3 Allow the ivy to climb up over the framework and then keep it trimmed in the same way as you would any topiary —by carefully clipping it over, using the frame as a guide.

COMPLICATED SHAPES

Intricate shapes, such as crowns or birds, need a great deal more planning. Before the shrub has grown too big, a former must be inserted inside it. This can be a metal frame, which will support any thin stems during their formative years. Without support, for example, a bird's tail might droop, grow upward, or even sideways. Metal is the best material, but a temporary former (which will eventually be taken out) can be made of wood.

LEFT *In winter, topiary must be protected from heavy snowfall, which might damage it.*

KEEPING IN SHAPE

It is difficult to cut accurately by eye, and even a simple shape like a ball will soon grow wildly out of shape. While the topiary is still growing and when fully grown, the internal former will act as a cutting guide so that the shape can be maintained. When you are trimming, keep to the same distance from the former in all directions.

An external former can also be made for trimming. For example, a wooden or wire framework can be dropped over the shape and the stems trimmed back to it. A simple cone can be made from three bamboo canes and hoops of wires the exact shape of the finished topiary. Such a former not only keeps individual plants in shape, but it can be used on different plants to ensure uniformity.

Complicated shapes are best trimmed with shears or even pruning shears. Avoid using power trimmers except with flat shapes, because the slightest deviation with the tip can result in unwanted dips and holes or even lost features. Using hand shears permits a more thoughtful cut.

When they are used as hedges, box and yew need trimming only once a year. Both plants do, despite their reputation, grow surprisingly quickly and the outline of a piece of topiary can be quickly obscured. It may be necessary to cut such a piece as often as every six weeks or so, although simple shapes need be cut only twice during the year.

GROWING EDIBLE PLANTS AGAINST WALLS

*I*n *a small garden it makes sense to grow fruit trees against the walls. The framework of the trees, whether they are grown as espaliers, fans, or cordons, is attractive, both in winter, when the outlines can be clearly seen, and in summer, when the branches are hidden by leaves. There are, in addition, the blossom and new leaves in spring, the fruit in summer or autumn, and, generally, the autumn color of the foliage. Several types of tree and soft fruits can be trained to grow on walls. Apples, pears, cherries, plums, figs, peaches, apricots, nectarines, red currants, and gooseberries can all be grown against a wall or a fence.*

Cane fruit, such as raspberries, blackberries, and black caps, is grown against wires stretched between posts. The techniques used to grow tree fruit against walls can also be used to grow them against post and wires.

FANS

Fans are suitable for most tree fruits and consist of a short trunk with branches fanning out from it. Plant a feathered maiden (a one-year-old tree with side branches) against a wall with horizontal wires 15in (38cm) apart. Cut just above a sideshoot, about 12in (60cm) from the ground. There should be a second sideshoot just below and on the other side of the main stem. Remove all other sideshoots below this. Fix canes to the wires (40° to the horizontal) and tie the two sideshoots to them. Reduce sideshoots to three buds about 15in (38cm) from their base.

The following summer, tie in the shoot from the top bud along the same cane to increase the length of the main sideshoot. The shoots from the two buds below this should be tied to canes that are set at about 40° to the main sideshoot. Remove all sideshoots below these. Continue in this manner until a complete fan has been established. As the shoots fruit, cut them back to a suitable replacement shoot, which should be tied into its place. Any shoots not required for replacement purposes should be cut back to four or five leaves.

CORDONS

There are various styles of cordon. A single cordon is basically a single pole of fruit set at 45° to the horizontal. Feathered maidens are planted in early spring and tied to a cane supported at 45° by the wires on the wall. Reduce all sideshoots to three or four buds. In summer any new

ABOVE *This attractive apple espalier has added charm in spring, when a mass of* blossoms snakes across the wall. Choose an apple variety suitable for training in this way.

growth on all the old sideshoots should be reduced to one leaf, and any new sideshoots should be reduced to three leaves. This procedure is continued year after year. If the spurs become overcrowded, cut out a few of the older shoots.

MULTIPLE CORDONS

Plant a maiden whip, and cut it off just above the first wire. The two shoots that appear at the top of the stem should be trained along bamboo canes held at 45°; the canes are lowered to 30° the following winter. Remove any sideshoots that appear below the top two. Once the sideshoots are 18in (45cm) apart, train them upwards and attach them to vertical canes. Remove all sideshoots on the sloping arms and train the vertical stems in the same way as for a single cordon, although this time they should be left upright.

PROJECT PLANTING AGAINST A WALL

1 Dig a hole at least 18in (45cm) away from the wall, making it wider than the plant. Place the plant in the hole, spreading out any loose roots. Fill in with soil.

2 Gently but firmly pack the soil down around the plant and water. Top-dress with bark or some other mulch. Cut out any weak or damaged shoots.

3 Place one or more shoots (depending on the number of remaining stems) against the supports. Tie the shoots to these. Allow for growth and do not tie too tightly.

PROJECT TRAINING AN ESPALIER

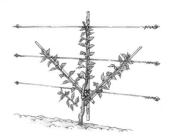

1 Espaliers consist of tree branches trained horizontally from a central trunk. They are very decorative. Attach wires to the wall using vine eye hooks. The wires should be about 15in (38cm) apart. Prepare the ground thoroughly for planting.

2 In early spring plant a maiden whip (a one-year-old with no side branches) of the desired fruit. Tie it in position against a cane and cut it off just above the wire, making sure that there are two strong buds below and one above.

3 In summer, train the new leader from the top bud onto the vertical cane. Tie the stems that have come from the next two buds to canes fixed to the wires at 45°. Any shoot below this should be removed back to the main stem.

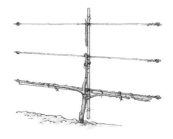

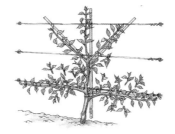

4 The next winter, reduce the leader to one bud above and two below the second wire. Lower the canes holding the two lower shoots into a horizontal position and tie to the wires. Remove a third of each shoot: cut above a downward-facing bud.

5 During the second summer repeat the first summer's procedure (see step 3), but this time with the second tier. Reduce the sideshoots that appear on branches of the first tier to three leaves. Continue with this method until all the tiers are complete.

6 It is possible to grow tall pear trees of up to ten tiers on the end wall of a house, but most espaliers are restricted to just two, three, or possibly, four tiers. When all the tiers have formed, prune in the same way as cordons.

WONDERFUL WALLS

A gardener who has walls is fortunate indeed. They can contribute so much to a garden's appearance, both as a background in their own right and as a support for plants. Most gardeners are at least blessed with house walls, and the really lucky ones have garden walls as well. It is, of course, always possible to build your own walls, at least on a modest scale, although large walls are expensive to build and require expert help.

Low walls are not too difficult to build, and the effort often turns out to be good fun. The walls can be freestanding structures, which will become part of a raised bed, or they may simply act as the edge of a patio. On the other hand, you may want a retaining wall that holds back a higher part of the garden. Walls higher than, say, 24in (60cm) need to be built well, and professional help should be sought if you are in any doubt about your ability.

FOUNDATIONS

All walls are best built on foundations; otherwise, they will crack as the ground shifts unevenly. Low walls in warm areas should have at least 15in (38cm) of foundation, (deeper in cold climates) consisting of about 5in (13cm) of rammed crushed stone covered with 4in (10cm) of concrete. The remainder of the foundation consists of the lower part of the wall that emerges from the ground. The rammed crushed stone and concrete foundations should be at least 4in (10cm) wider than the wall.

BUILDING A WALL

Walls can be built of brick or concrete blocks. The blocks can be either rather rough or made with a sandy coloring

ABOVE *A raised bed is an opportunity to add interesting texture to the garden.*

and textured surface that resembles stone. The bricks or blocks are laid on a thin bed of cement in such a way that one row of bricks overlaps the previous row. If the wall is low—up to 18–24in (45–60cm)—it can be a single brick thick, but a more sturdy wall, and one that is more attractive, is made with a double layer of bricks or the equivalent thickness of blocks. The top layer of a double-thickness wall is usually finished with a row of bricks laid on their sides across the wall. This not only bonds both sides together but also produces a pleasing "capping" effect. On a block wall, slabs are often used for the top layer, and when these are slightly wider than the wall, a capped effect is achieved.

PLANTING IN DRYSTONE WALLS

There is often enough dust and detritus lurking in the cracks of the vertical faces of a drystone wall to enable plants to survive there. Obviously, you must select plants

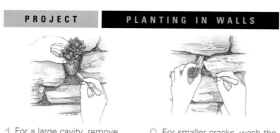

PROJECT	PLANTING IN WALLS

1 For a large cavity, remove the plant from its pot and gently squeeze the root ball into an oval shape. Insert and water.

2 For smaller cracks, wash the soil off the roots, wrap in a piece of wet tissue, insert. Trickle soil over the roots.

that are used to dry conditions, such as wallflowers, as there is often very little moisture available. Rock-garden plants that enjoy good drainage will also flourish. Suitable mat-forming plants include *Gypsophila repens* and *Saponaria ocymoides*. Hens and chickens (*Sempervivum*) also look good.

SOWING SEEDS IN A DRYSTONE WALL

It is often difficult to get plants established in the vertical faces of a wall, especially if the crevices are narrow. However, if plenty of seed is placed in the cracks then some at least will usually germinate. The difficulty is getting fine seed into the cracks—see the project instructions.

MOSAICS

Mosaics can add wonderful colors to a garden, brightening it up all the year round, even during the dull days of winter. Quality mosaic tiles (tesserae) can be purchased from specialty craft shops, but there are plenty of pieces of broken pottery, mirrors, tiles, shells, glass, and other things that can be used. Larger pieces of pottery, plates and cups for example, can be broken down to smaller pieces using a standard tile cutter. The shapes need not be regular. The design can be copied from a book or simply made up. It can be figurative, perhaps a picture of a bird, for example, or it can be entirely abstract. Creating a pattern is usually better than just applying the pieces at random, but even this can create an attractive picture.

HINTS AND TIPS

🖐 Most walls, even very low ones, need solid foundations if they are to remain upright and not crack.

🖐 Stone blocks can be very heavy to move, so, if using them to build a wall, always get help.

🖐 High walls can be dangerous if not properly built. Employ a qualified builder if you are in doubt of your own ability.

🖐 Never attach mosaics directly to the wall if you want to take them with you when you move. Create them on waterproof board.

PROJECT — SEEDS IN WALLS

 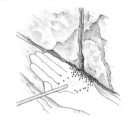

1 Place some seed on the palm of your left hand and position it level with the cracks that you wish to seed.

2 Place the tip of a drinking straw on the palm of your hand, just behind the seeds, and blow through it, the jet of air directing the seed into the crevice. Now just let nature take over.

PROJECT — MOSAICS

1 Clean the wall, brushing off all loose pieces and dust. If it has deep indentations, fill these with cement. Seal the area to be covered with a special sealer used to prime exterior walls before painting.

2 Transfer your design from a preliminary sketch on paper to the wall. If the design is complicated, draw a grid on both the wall and drawing and use this as a guide.

3 Using a waterproof adhesive, mixed to the manufacturer's instructions, start to apply the mosaics, filling in one section at a time.

4 Once the adhesive has cured and the pieces are stuck firm, work a grout over the whole surface to fill the gaps. Wipe the mosaic several times until all grout is removed from the surface of the pieces.

ARBORS

*I*t is important to remember that one of the main functions of a garden is to provide pleasure, and there is no better way of enjoying your garden than relaxing in a shady arbor surrounded by scented plants. Arbors are not difficult structures to make, and it is possible to purchase kits from garden centers. The better ones are made of metal.

Buy the largest structure you can afford—the inside dimensions of an arbor shrink considerably once it is covered with climbers sending shoots in all directions.

You can also easily make your own structure. The simplest arbor is a rustic style made from poles, which will not only look romantic when covered with climbers but is also easy for beginners and nonwoodworkers to make, because any mistakes will add to the rustic charm. A more formal structure can be made from trellising.

RUSTIC SIMPLICITY

This type of arbor can be made with irregular poles or with squared-up timber. If you use poles, you will find it easier to nail one piece to another if the two rounded surfaces that will make contact have been flattened with a chisel. A proper joint is not necessary as long as the two surfaces fit snugly against each another.

If you use squared-up timber, the various pieces can be nailed together or jointed for extra strength. Do not cut too far into the main timbers, or they will be considerably weakened. A shallow joint is all that is needed, and the two pieces of wood need not sit flush with each other.

The wood, and hence the structure, will last much longer if it is treated with a preservative. The critical place is the point where the post enters the ground. Make sure this is well soaked in preservative. Avoid using creosote, because contact with it and its fumes will kill not only the climbers but possibly other plants in the vicinity.

A structure covered with climbers is like the sail of a ship and will have to withstand tremendous wind pressure. It is important, therefore, to use stout posts and to bury them well in the ground. They can be placed in a hole and the earth rammed back around them, but a more secure method is to fill the hole with concrete. The top of the concrete should be just below soil level so that it

can be hidden with soil. Also, it should slope away from the post so that water runs away.

A FORMAL ARBOR

A more formal structure can be created by erecting the posts in the same manner but by filling the sides, back, and top with panels of trellising. This is readily available at garden centers and usually has a square design, although diamond patterns can also be found. The regular pattern of the trellis will show even when it is covered with climbers, making a pleasing contrast to the vegetation.

SUMMERHOUSES

If you would rather keep the climbers at arm's length (you may be frightened of insects or spiders), there is no reason why you should not buy or build an open summerhouse, which will have at least one open side, and cover this with climbers. You will get the benefit of the fragrance without the worry of unwelcome things dropping on you. There is the added advantage that you can sit in it in the rain.

RIGHT *Do not neglect the climbers on an arbor—they must be trained and pruned just like any other climbing plant.*

PLANTING THE ARBOR

Any climbers can be used to cover an arbor, but scented ones are obviously best. There are many roses to choose from, but *R. 'Zéphirine Drouhin'* is a winner because not only does it have a long season but it is also thornless, an important advantage in a confined space. *Clematis montana*, with its vanilla scent, is good for spring. Honeysuckles come next in season, although the glorious red form *Lonicera periclymenum* 'Serotina' carries through well into late summer. Jasmine offers a strong evening scent for late summer. Shrubs such as philadelphus and lilac can be planted nearby to add to the perfumes.

PROJECT **READY-MADE ARBOR**

1 Buy a metal arbor kit and erect it. Those available may be small, so make sure that you buy one that is big enough.

2 Plant with scented climbers in early spring, adding well-rotted organic matter. Keep well watered.

PROJECT **A RUSTIC ARBOR**

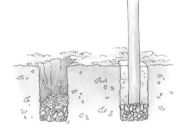

1 Draw a rough sketch of what you are going to create to get an idea of what you will need. Make sure that it is large enough to accommodate a bench, bearing in mind that the climbers will grow out by at least 12in (30cm) from their supports.

2 Dig four holes, each 24in (60cm) deep, for the corners. Place 6in (15cm) of rubble at the bottom, then insert the posts, checking that they are vertical with a level, before filling in with concrete.

3 Use galvanized nails to fix horizontal crossbars along the sides and back at 12in (30cm) intervals. For a stronger structure, cut notches in the posts to take the bars. Alternatively, nail one piece directly to the other.

4 To make the roof, lay two posts on the ground and connect them with crossbars. Make another set and attach the two with another crossbar to make a pitched roof. Lift the roof into position and nail it to the top of the frame.

5 Plant roses, honeysuckle, and jasmine around the arbor and tie the young shoots to the framework.

6 As the plants grow, tie them in so that eventually the whole arbor is covered with scented climbers. Place a bench or seat inside the arbor.

TRELLISES

Trellising is perfect for creating screens or simply for adding height to parts of the garden. They can be used in their own right, without any adornment, but most gardeners use them as an opportunity to grow even more roses, clematis, and other climbers. They are not particularly difficult to erect and you can even make your own. When they are erected carefully, they should give years of pleasure.

The secret of good trellising is to make sure that the main poles are securly anchored. When it is covered in climbers, trellis is subjected to considerable wind forces, and unless the posts are concreted into the ground they are liable to be blown over. Even what may seem as solidly compacted soil will yield to wind pressure, especially if it is accompanied by rain that softens the earth. For the same reasons the wood must be sound, and free from knots and splits.

Treat all wood with a preservative (not creosote). The point at which the posts enter the ground is especially vulnerable, so give the base of all posts a good soaking.

FORMAL TRELLISES

A wide selection of panels can be bought from garden centers. Most trellis is supplied in a natural color. It can be stained or, if it has not been treated with preservative and is therefore oily, it can be painted.

It is possible to buy, or to make, matching obelisks or pyramids to place in the beds. These help to unite the borders with the trellis, making a whole picture.

RUSTIC TRELLISES

A rustic trellis is made from round poles that have not been processed; they are, therefore, not uniformly straight but still have a few kinks and bends in them. Although they look even more rustic with their bark on, it is always best to remove the bark, because water can remain below it after rain and cause the wood to rot. Use stout poles for the uprights, with slightly thinner ones for the crosspieces.

Any number of different patterns can be used. The style illustrated does not go right to the ground, but there is no reason why it should not. The panels can be divided up in different ways, with a combination of horizontal, vertical, and diagonal rails. Whatever style is selected, remember that the rails should serve three main functions: they must strengthen the trellis, provide support for climbers, and be decorative in their own right.

It is possible to buy rustic trellising in panel form. This may be cheaper and better made than trellis you could make yourself, but it may not be, so look at it carefully.

LEFT *Ask a friend to help you erect trellis. The joints will be more secure if one person holds the panels as the other secures them, and construction injuries are less likely!*

FORMAL TRELLISES

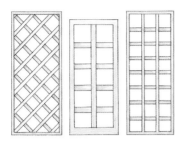

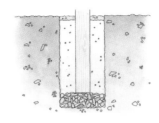

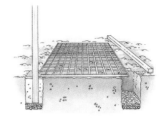

1 A wide selection of trellis panels is available from garden centers. Some are flimsier than others. Measure the site beforehand to find out how many you need.

2 Dig a hole 24in (60cm) deep and place 4in (10cm) of rubble in the base. Insert the pole and fill up to just below the soil level with a dry-mix concrete.

3 Lay the panel on the ground to check where the next post will go, and dig a hole. Place rubble in the bottom of it. (Do not put the post in position.)

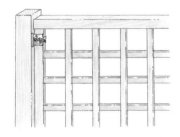

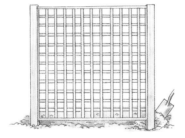

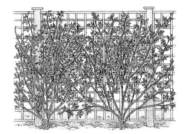

4 Ask someone to help you hold the panel against the first post and fix it in position with special clips or with galvanized nails. It is usually best to drill pilot holes in the panel first so that the wood does not split.

5 While the unattached end of the panel is supported by your helper, put the post in the hole and place it against the panel. Fix the panel to the post, and then fill in the hole with a dry concrete mix, making sure that the post is upright and the panel is level.

6 Dig the next post hole and continue as in step 5 until the whole trellis is finished. Plant climbers at any point along the trellis, spreading the shoots out so that the whole trellis is covered.

RUSTIC TRELLIS

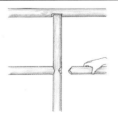

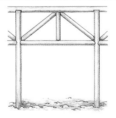

1 Dig all the post holes (*see step 2 above*), but this time secure all the vertical posts in place with concrete. Nail rails across the top of the posts, halving the joints where they cross the uprights.

2 Use a bird's-mouth joint (a notch in the upright and equivalent shape on the end of the rail) to fix a horizontal rail between the uprights, two-thirds of the way up from ground level.

3 Halfway between the main uprights, insert a vertical post between the rails and add two diagonal crossbraces. Repeat the process along the whole trellis.

4 Plant roses and clematis next to the posts. Lead the shoots up to the first crossbar and spread them out so that the trellis becomes covered.

THE PLANT DIRECTORY

The essence of any garden is, of course, the plants. The following pages detail some of the many plants that draw the eye upward, emphasizing the vertical element. Browse through these and use the notes and pictures, along with your own observations when you visit gardens, to make your choice.

LEFT *Vertical threads of* Verbascum *and* Lychnis coronaria, *stitched through with* Rosa *'Festival', weave into a leafy canvas of golden hop.*

HOW TO USE THIS DIRECTORY

The Plant Directory lists all the plants that are featured in this book, together with a selection of other plants that are suitable for adding height to a garden. It is not intended to be exhaustive, and experienced gardeners will have their own favorites. However, this listing has been made with the specific requirements of a vertical garden in mind, and will guide the beginner to a range of attractive and readily available plants, shrubs, and trees with which to create a beautiful garden. Complete information on planting and maintaining the plants is given for each entry.

The Plant Directory is divided into different categories that group various types of plant together for easy reference. The directory encompasses plants that perform in different seasons, giving you the opportunity to create a vertical garden that remains interesting the whole year round. From the basic framework of trees and shrubs to the more ornamental touches of flowers, there is a wealth of plants to inspire your creative flair. The plant categories are annuals and biennials *(page 64)*, herbaceous perennials *(page 66)*, shrubs *(page 68)*, climbers *(page 78)*, trees and conifers *(page 104)*, and fruit *(page 106)*. The symbols panel accompanying each entry gives essential information on the growing conditions required to ensure the plant's health and productivity.

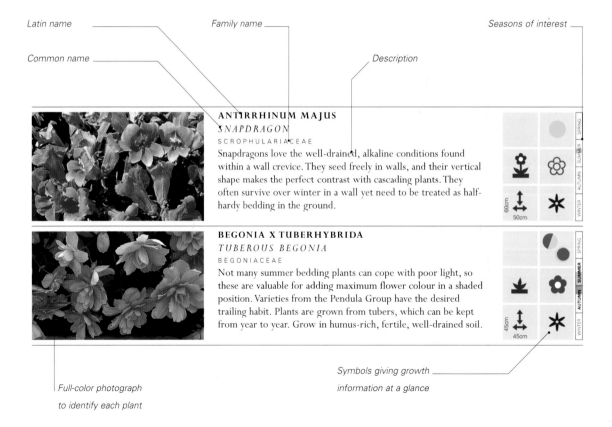

Latin name

Common name

Family name

Description

Seasons of interest

ANTIRRHINUM MAJUS
SNAPDRAGON
SCROPHULARIACEAE
Snapdragons love the well-drained, alkaline conditions found within a wall crevice. They seed freely in walls, and their vertical shape makes the perfect contrast with cascading plants. They often survive over winter in a wall yet need to be treated as half-hardy bedding in the ground.

BEGONIA X TUBERHYBRIDA
TUBEROUS BEGONIA
BEGONIACEAE
Not many summer bedding plants can cope with poor light, so these are valuable for adding maximum flower colour in a shaded position. Varieties from the Pendula Group have the desired trailing habit. Plants are grown from tubers, which can be kept from year to year. Grow in humus-rich, fertile, well-drained soil.

Full-color photograph to identify each plant

Symbols giving growth information at a glance

KEY TO THE SYMBOLS

 EASY TO GROW

These are tolerant plants that require no special care or conditions in order to flourish.

 MODERATE TO GROW

These are plants that require some special care, such as protection from frost.

 DIFFICULT TO GROW

These are plants that require a great deal of specialized care, and offer a challenge for the more experienced gardener.

 EVERGREEN

 SEMIEVERGREEN

 DECIDUOUS

Deciduous plants lose all their leaves in autumn (sometimes in summer), while evergreen plants keep their foliage all year. Plants described as semievergreen may keep some or all of their foliage through the winter in sheltered gardens or if the weather is mild. No leaf symbol is given for annuals, nor for biennials, although some biennials do keep their leaves over the first winter.

 FEATURE LEAVES

 FEATURE SCENT

 FEATURE FLOWER

 FEATURE FRUIT

These symbols indicate the main feature of interest for each plant in the directory, although this is not necessarily the plant's only attractive asset. Some plants are given more than one symbol. This information will help you to choose plants that have complementary features, or plants that will perform a specific function in your garden.

 RAPID GROWTH

 MODERATE GROWTH

 SLOW GROWTH

Speed of growth is a highly subjective category, and will vary according to local conditions. Rapid growth indicates plants that reach their full extent in a single season, or plants that make substantial progress toward filling the space allowed for them in a single season. Slow growth indicates plants that take several seasons to reach their ultimate size. Moderate growth refers to rates of progress between these two extremes.

SEASON OF INTEREST

The period of the year when a plant is likely to be most attractive is also indicated (those plants that have something to offer all year round are marked accordingly). This will help you in creating a planting plan for each season.

HARDINESS ZONES

An indication of the frost-hardiness of each plant is given (a zone map can be found on page 112). In the case of annuals and tender perennials, you should check with your supplier to make sure you can offer the plant the right growing conditions.

 HEIGHT AND SPREAD

The size of plants will vary according to the growing conditions in your garden, so these measurements are a rough guide only. The measurements refer to the size of plants and trees when mature, although there are specific circumstances where the ultimate size is never reached.

 FULL SUN

 PARTIAL SUN

 SHADE

An indication of light preference is given to show each plant's optimum growing situation. Here again, this is only a rough guide, as some plants that prefer sun may also be reasonably tolerant of shade.

ANNUALS AND BIENNIALS

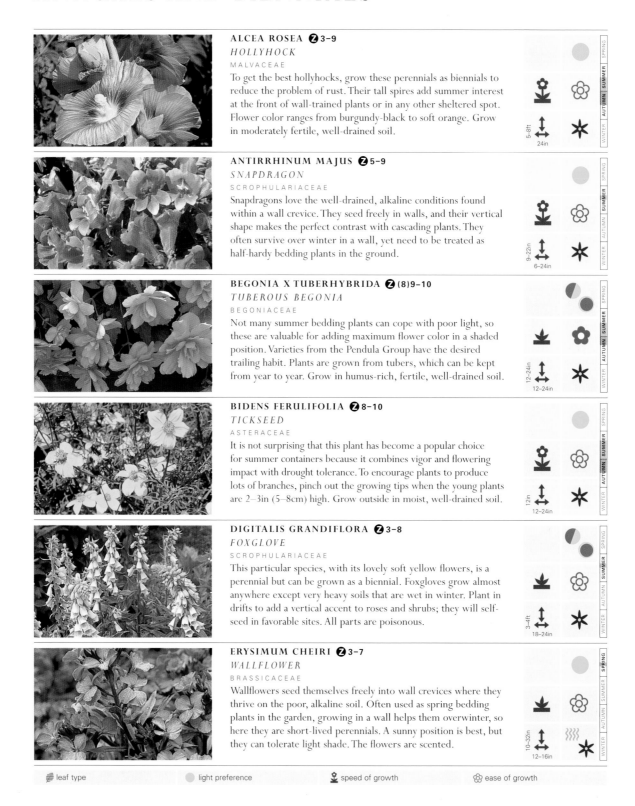

ALCEA ROSEA ❷ 3–9
HOLLYHOCK
MALVACEAE

To get the best hollyhocks, grow these perennials as biennials to reduce the problem of rust. Their tall spires add summer interest at the front of wall-trained plants or in any other sheltered spot. Flower color ranges from burgundy-black to soft orange. Grow in moderately fertile, well-drained soil.

5–8ft
24in

ANTIRRHINUM MAJUS ❷ 5–9
SNAPDRAGON
SCROPHULARIACEAE

Snapdragons love the well-drained, alkaline conditions found within a wall crevice. They seed freely in walls, and their vertical shape makes the perfect contrast with cascading plants. They often survive over winter in a wall, yet need to be treated as half-hardy bedding plants in the ground.

9–22in
6–24in

BEGONIA X TUBERHYBRIDA ❷ (8)9–10
TUBEROUS BEGONIA
BEGONIACEAE

Not many summer bedding plants can cope with poor light, so these are valuable for adding maximum flower color in a shaded position. Varieties from the Pendula Group have the desired trailing habit. Plants are grown from tubers, which can be kept from year to year. Grow in humus-rich, fertile, well-drained soil.

12–24in
12–24in

BIDENS FERULIFOLIA ❷ 8–10
TICKSEED
ASTERACEAE

It is not surprising that this plant has become a popular choice for summer containers because it combines vigor and flowering impact with drought tolerance. To encourage plants to produce lots of branches, pinch out the growing tips when the young plants are 2–3in (5–8cm) high. Grow outside in moist, well-drained soil.

12in
12–24in

DIGITALIS GRANDIFLORA ❷ 3–8
FOXGLOVE
SCROPHULARIACEAE

This particular species, with its lovely soft yellow flowers, is a perennial but can be grown as a biennial. Foxgloves grow almost anywhere except very heavy soils that are wet in winter. Plant in drifts to add a vertical accent to roses and shrubs; they will self-seed in favorable sites. All parts are poisonous.

3–4ft
18–24in

ERYSIMUM CHEIRI ❷ 3–7
WALLFLOWER
BRASSICACEAE

Wallflowers seed themselves freely into wall crevices where they thrive on the poor, alkaline soil. Often used as spring bedding plants in the garden, growing in a wall helps them overwinter, so here they are short-lived perennials. A sunny position is best, but they can tolerate light shade. The flowers are scented.

10–32in
12–16in

SPRING · SUMMER · AUTUMN · WINTER

🌿 leaf type   ● light preference   🌱 speed of growth   ❀ ease of growth

HELIANTHUS ANNUUS 2–11
SUNFLOWER
ASTERACEAE

This plant is grown for its large daisy—like flowerheads, which are yellow—sometimes colored with touches of red and purple. It is a fast-growing plant with a hairy stem and toothed, heart-shaped green leaves. Will thrive against a wall or in a border, as long as the soil is fertile, humus-rich, moist, but well drained.

15ft / 24–36in

LOTUS BERTHELOTII 9–10
PARROT'S BEAK
PAPILIONACEAE

The cascades of feathery, silver foliage are the main attraction—regard any red or orange flowers as a bonus because they are produced only in hot summers or on older plants. It is a tender shrub, but can be used as a summer bedding plant by taking cuttings in summer. Grow in moderately fertile, well-drained soil.

8in / 3–4ft

OENOTHERA BIENNIS 4–8
EVENING PRIMROSE
ONAGRACEAE

An upright annual usually grown as a biennial. Its oval leaves, with red outlines, are attractive but secondary to the bowl-shaped yellow flowers borne between summer and autumn. Requires moderately fertile, moist soil to do well. The seeds are used to make the popular evening primrose oil.

3–5ft / 24in

PELARGONIUM PELTATUM 9–10
IVY-LEAVED GERANIUM
GERANIACEAE

The foliage is shaped like ivy, but the leaf color varies from a glossy green to variegated. Some varieties, like *P.* 'The Crocodile', have attractive veined leaves. Use as a single subject for hanging baskets or wall planters. The flowers and foliage are more tolerant of weather than most pelargoniums.

12in / 6–48in

PETUNIA 2–9
TRAILING PETUNIA
SOLANACEAE

Trailing petunias are a recent addition to summer container planting, which became really popular when the Surfinia type was introduced in the mid-1990s. Now there are many others to choose from. Grow as a single subject in light, well-drained soil, and water and feed regularly.

8–16in / 12–36in

VERBASCUM BOMBYCIFERUM 4–8
MULLEIN
SCROPHULARIACEAE

An attractive biennial with a strong vertical shape. Leaves are woolly-white and of an oblong shape. In summer, the plant carries saucer-shaped, dark yellow flowers in branched spikes. Best in alkaline, poor, well-drained soil. If grown in fertile soil, it will grow to a greater height and will require some form of support.

8ft / 24–40in

---

 height and spread   ✳ feature of interest   ▦ season of interest   *ANNUALS AND BIENNIALS* ***A – V***

HERBACEOUS PERENNIALS

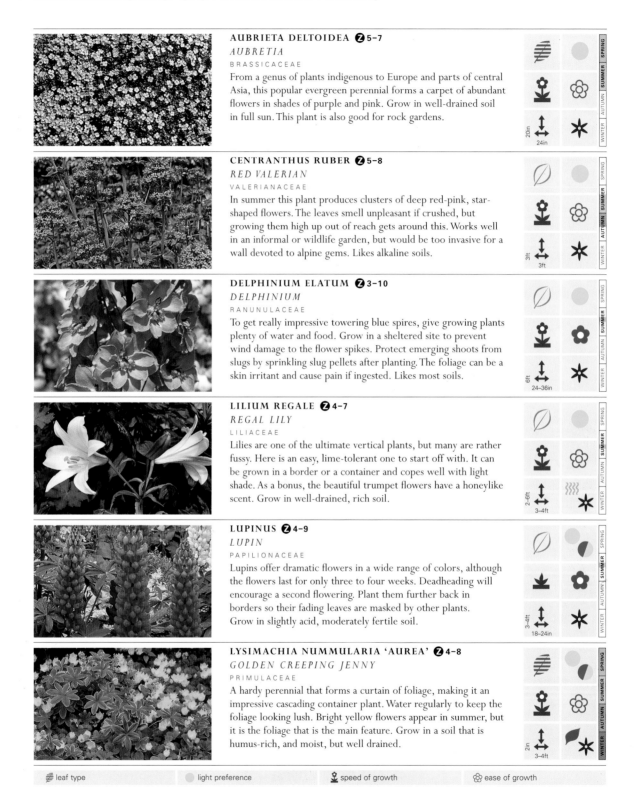

AUBRIETA DELTOIDEA ❷ 5–7

AUBRETIA

BRASSICACEAE

From a genus of plants indigenous to Europe and parts of central Asia, this popular evergreen perennial forms a carpet of abundant flowers in shades of purple and pink. Grow in well-drained soil in full sun. This plant is also good for rock gardens.

20in / 24in

CENTRANTHUS RUBER ❷ 5–8

RED VALERIAN

VALERIANACEAE

In summer this plant produces clusters of deep red-pink, star-shaped flowers. The leaves smell unpleasant if crushed, but growing them high up out of reach gets around this. Works well in an informal or wildlife garden, but would be too invasive for a wall devoted to alpine gems. Likes alkaline soils.

3ft / 3ft

DELPHINIUM ELATUM ❷ 3–10

DELPHINIUM

RANUNULACEAE

To get really impressive towering blue spires, give growing plants plenty of water and food. Grow in a sheltered site to prevent wind damage to the flower spikes. Protect emerging shoots from slugs by sprinkling slug pellets after planting. The foliage can be a skin irritant and cause pain if ingested. Likes most soils.

6ft / 24–36in

LILIUM REGALE ❷ 4–7

REGAL LILY

LILIACEAE

Lilies are one of the ultimate vertical plants, but many are rather fussy. Here is an easy, lime-tolerant one to start off with. It can be grown in a border or a container and copes well with light shade. As a bonus, the beautiful trumpet flowers have a honeylike scent. Grow in well-drained, rich soil.

2–6ft / 3–4ft

LUPINUS ❷ 4–9

LUPIN

PAPILIONACEAE

Lupins offer dramatic flowers in a wide range of colors, although the flowers last for only three to four weeks. Deadheading will encourage a second flowering. Plant them further back in borders so their fading leaves are masked by other plants. Grow in slightly acid, moderately fertile soil.

3–4ft / 18–24in

LYSIMACHIA NUMMULARIA 'AUREA' ❷ 4–8

GOLDEN CREEPING JENNY

PRIMULACEAE

A hardy perennial that forms a curtain of foliage, making it an impressive cascading container plant. Water regularly to keep the foliage looking lush. Bright yellow flowers appear in summer, but it is the foliage that is the main feature. Grow in a soil that is humus-rich, and moist, but well drained.

2in / 3–4ft

≣ leaf type   ● light preference   ⚓ speed of growth   ✿ ease of growth

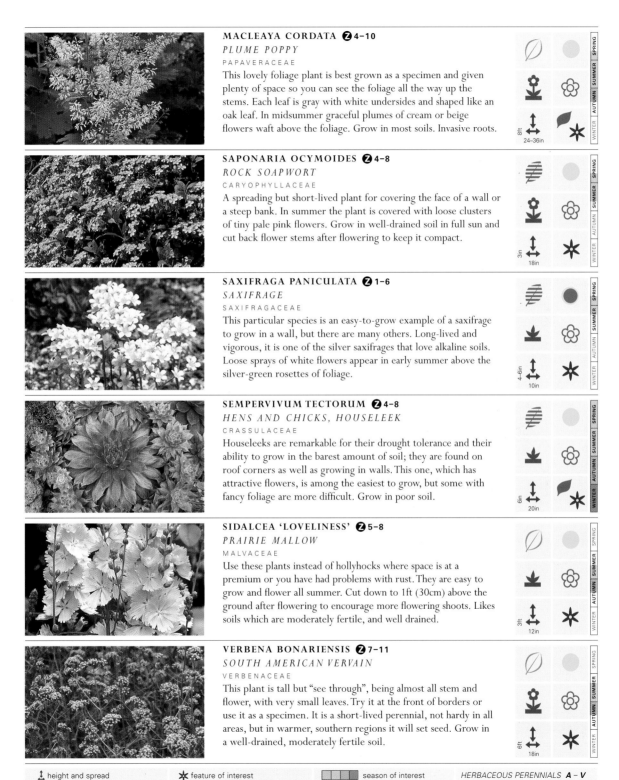

MACLEAYA CORDATA Z 4–10
PLUME POPPY
PAPAVERACEAE

This lovely foliage plant is best grown as a specimen and given plenty of space so you can see the foliage all the way up the stems. Each leaf is gray with white undersides and shaped like an oak leaf. In midsummer graceful plumes of cream or beige flowers waft above the foliage. Grow in most soils. Invasive roots.

8ft
24–36in

SAPONARIA OCYMOIDES Z 4–8
ROCK SOAPWORT
CARYOPHYLLACEAE

A spreading but short-lived plant for covering the face of a wall or a steep bank. In summer the plant is covered with loose clusters of tiny pale pink flowers. Grow in well-drained soil in full sun and cut back flower stems after flowering to keep it compact.

3in
18in

SAXIFRAGA PANICULATA Z 1–6
SAXIFRAGE
SAXIFRAGACEAE

This particular species is an easy-to-grow example of a saxifrage to grow in a wall, but there are many others. Long-lived and vigorous, it is one of the silver saxifrages that love alkaline soils. Loose sprays of white flowers appear in early summer above the silver-green rosettes of foliage.

4–6in
10in

SEMPERVIVUM TECTORUM Z 4–8
HENS AND CHICKS, HOUSELEEK
CRASSULACEAE

Houseleeks are remarkable for their drought tolerance and their ability to grow in the barest amount of soil; they are found on roof corners as well as growing in walls. This one, which has attractive flowers, is among the easiest to grow, but some with fancy foliage are more difficult. Grow in poor soil.

6in
20in

SIDALCEA 'LOVELINESS' Z 5–8
PRAIRIE MALLOW
MALVACEAE

Use these plants instead of hollyhocks where space is at a premium or you have had problems with rust. They are easy to grow and flower all summer. Cut down to 1ft (30cm) above the ground after flowering to encourage more flowering shoots. Likes soils which are moderately fertile, and well drained.

3ft
12in

VERBENA BONARIENSIS Z 7–11
SOUTH AMERICAN VERVAIN
VERBENACEAE

This plant is tall but "see through", being almost all stem and flower, with very small leaves. Try it at the front of borders or use it as a specimen. It is a short-lived perennial, not hardy in all areas, but in warmer, southern regions it will set seed. Grow in a well-drained, moderately fertile soil.

6ft
18in

↨ height and spread	✳ feature of interest	▢▢▢▢ season of interest	*HERBACEOUS PERENNIALS* **A – V**

SHRUBS

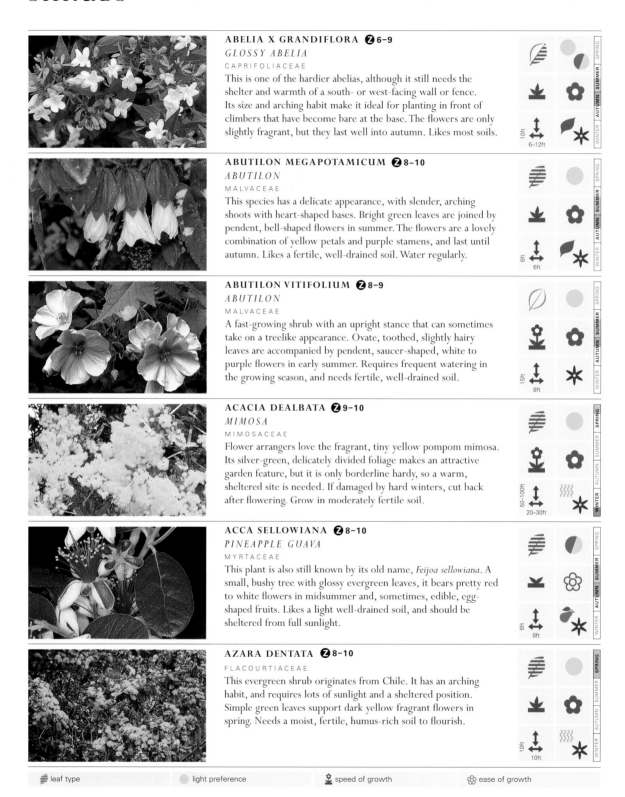

ABELIA X GRANDIFLORA ⓩ 6–9
GLOSSY ABELIA
CAPRIFOLIACEAE

This is one of the hardier abelias, although it still needs the shelter and warmth of a south- or west-facing wall or fence. Its size and arching habit make it ideal for planting in front of climbers that have become bare at the base. The flowers are only slightly fragrant, but they last well into autumn. Likes most soils.

ABUTILON MEGAPOTAMICUM ⓩ 8–10
ABUTILON
MALVACEAE

This species has a delicate appearance, with slender, arching shoots with heart-shaped bases. Bright green leaves are joined by pendent, bell-shaped flowers in summer. The flowers are a lovely combination of yellow petals and purple stamens, and last until autumn. Likes a fertile, well-drained soil. Water regularly.

ABUTILON VITIFOLIUM ⓩ 8–9
ABUTILON
MALVACEAE

A fast-growing shrub with an upright stance that can sometimes take on a treelike appearance. Ovate, toothed, slightly hairy leaves are accompanied by pendent, saucer-shaped, white to purple flowers in early summer. Requires frequent watering in the growing season, and needs fertile, well-drained soil.

ACACIA DEALBATA ⓩ 9–10
MIMOSA
MIMOSACEAE

Flower arrangers love the fragrant, tiny yellow pompom mimosa. Its silver-green, delicately divided foliage makes an attractive garden feature, but it is only borderline hardy, so a warm, sheltered site is needed. If damaged by hard winters, cut back after flowering. Grow in moderately fertile soil.

ACCA SELLOWIANA ⓩ 8–10
PINEAPPLE GUAVA
MYRTACEAE

This plant is also still known by its old name, *Feijoa sellowiana*. A small, bushy tree with glossy evergreen leaves, it bears pretty red to white flowers in midsummer and, sometimes, edible, egg-shaped fruits. Likes a light well-drained soil, and should be sheltered from full sunlight.

AZARA DENTATA ⓩ 8–10
FLACOURTIACEAE

This evergreen shrub originates from Chile. It has an arching habit, and requires lots of sunlight and a sheltered position. Simple green leaves support dark yellow fragrant flowers in spring. Needs a moist, fertile, humus-rich soil to flourish.

🌿 leaf type	⬤ light preference	🌱 speed of growth	✿ ease of growth

BUDDLEJA ALTERNIFOLIA ❷ 6-9

BUDDLEJACEAE

Earlier known as *Buddleia alternifolia*, this deciduous shrub or small tree has narrow, lance-shaped, pale green leaves. The small, lavender-blue flowers are borne in rounded clusters on arching branches in early summer. They have a sweet fragrance, with a slight bouquet of heliotrope. Grow in fertile, well-drained soil. It makes an ideal specimen plant.

12ft
12ft

BUDDLEJA CRISPA ❷ 8-9

BUDDLEIA

BUDDLEJACEAE

This is a choice buddleia with white, feltlike young stems and foliage. Not reliably hardy, it needs the shelter of a south-facing wall or fence. In late summer the fragrant lilac flowers attract butterflies just as its more common relative the butterfly bush (*B. davidii*). Grow in fertile, well-drained soil.

10ft
10ft

BUPLEURUM FRUTICOSUM ❷ 7-10

SHRUBBY HARE'S EAR

APIACEAE

An attractive evergreen shrub for exposed or coastal gardens, it is moderately hardy and is a good shrub for a warm wall. The glossy, blue-green leaves and shrubby habit make a good contrasting shape with strong vertical plants. Clusters of green-yellow flowers are borne in summer. Likes most soils.

6ft
8ft

BUXUS SEMPERVIRENS ❷ 6-8

BOX

BUXACEAE

Even the smallest garden has room for a clipped box spiral or pyramid; grow them in a container for a movable vertical shape. Box is very tolerant of all sites and soils, but aim to grow them well, because they are specimen plants. Clip with shears in midsummer and again in mid-autumn.

15ft
15ft

CALLISTEMON CITRINUS 'SPLENDENS' ❷ 10-11

BOTTLEBRUSH

MYRTACEAE

An interesting plant with distinctive bright red flowers, and leaves that emit a lemon scent when crushed. It is well worth trying against a south- or southwest-facing wall or fence or in a mild coastal area. In cold gardens grow it as a conservatory plant. Grow in acid, moist, but well-drained soil.

6-25ft
5-20ft

CAMELLIA JAPONICA ❷ 7-8

COMMON CAMELLIA

THEACEAE

Part of a genus of over 250 species of long-lived shrubs and trees, this variety is an upright to spreading shrub with glossy, dark green leaves and single red flowers. A good choice for year-round interest, as it flowers early in spring. Grow in moist, but well-drained, humus-rich, acid soil and mulch regularly.

10-20ft
3-10ft

 height and spread ✴ feature of interest ▭ season of interest *SHRUBS* **A – C**

SHRUBS

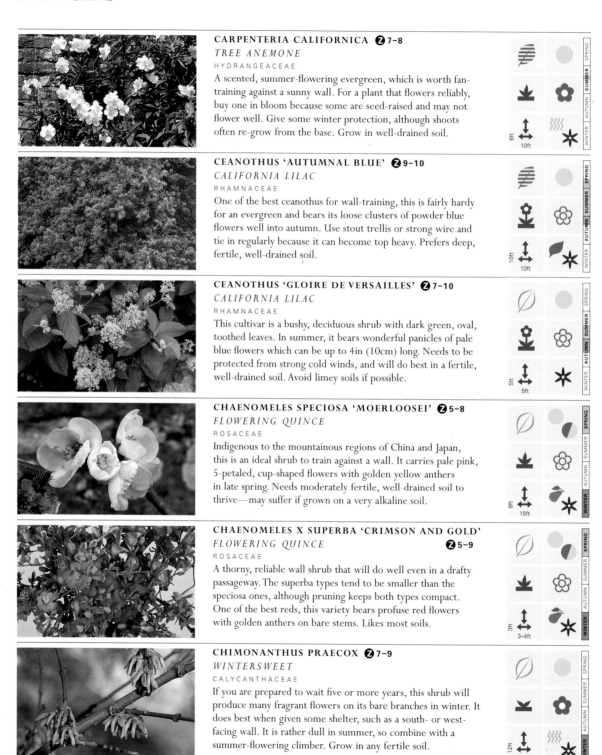

CARPENTERIA CALIFORNICA Z7–8
TREE ANEMONE

HYDRANGEACEAE

A scented, summer-flowering evergreen, which is worth fan-training against a sunny wall. For a plant that flowers reliably, buy one in bloom because some are seed-raised and may not flower well. Give some winter protection, although shoots often re-grow from the base. Grow in well-drained soil.

6ft 10ft

CEANOTHUS 'AUTUMNAL BLUE' Z9–10
CALIFORNIA LILAC

RHAMNACEAE

One of the best ceanothus for wall-training, this is fairly hardy for an evergreen and bears its loose clusters of powder blue flowers well into autumn. Use stout trellis or strong wire and tie in regularly because it can become top heavy. Prefers deep, fertile, well-drained soil.

10ft 10ft

CEANOTHUS 'GLOIRE DE VERSAILLES' Z7–10
CALIFORNIA LILAC

RHAMNACEAE

This cultivar is a bushy, deciduous shrub with dark green, oval, toothed leaves. In summer, it bears wonderful panicles of pale blue flowers which can be up to 4in (10cm) long. Needs to be protected from strong cold winds, and will do best in a fertile, well-drained soil. Avoid limey soils if possible.

5ft 5ft

CHAENOMELES SPECIOSA 'MOERLOOSEI' Z5–8
FLOWERING QUINCE

ROSACEAE

Indigenous to the mountainous regions of China and Japan, this is an ideal shrub to train against a wall. It carries pale pink, 5-petaled, cup-shaped flowers with golden yellow anthers in late spring. Needs moderately fertile, well-drained soil to thrive—may suffer if grown on a very alkaline soil.

8ft 15ft

CHAENOMELES X SUPERBA 'CRIMSON AND GOLD'
FLOWERING QUINCE Z5–9

ROSACEAE

A thorny, reliable wall shrub that will do well even in a drafty passageway. The superba types tend to be smaller than the speciosa ones, although pruning keeps both types compact. One of the best reds, this variety bears profuse red flowers with golden anthers on bare stems. Likes most soils.

3ft 3–4ft

CHIMONANTHUS PRAECOX Z7–9
WINTERSWEET

CALYCANTHACEAE

If you are prepared to wait five or more years, this shrub will produce many fragrant flowers on its bare branches in winter. It does best when given some shelter, such as a south- or west-facing wall. It is rather dull in summer, so combine with a summer-flowering climber. Grow in any fertile soil.

12ft 10ft

leaf type | light preference | speed of growth | ease of growth

CHOISYA TERNATA ❷8–10
MEXICAN ORANGE BLOSSOM
RUTACEAE

The sweet-scented flowers and glossy evergreen foliage make this shrub a popular choice. It is not at all fussy as long as it is sheltered from cold winds. In addition to the species, there is C. 'Aztec Pearl' with finely divided foliage but less scent, and C. t. 'Sundance', a yellow foliage shrub often grown against walls.

8ft / 8ft

COROKIA VIRGATA ❷8–10
CORNACEAE

This upright shrub has attractive, inversely lance-shaped leaves which are dark green above and white underneath. Ovoid yellow or orange fruit follow clusters of small, fragrant yellow flowers in late spring. Does best in a sheltered area or against a wall. Choose fertile, well-drained soil.

10ft / 10ft

CORONILLA VALENTINA SUBSP. GLAUCA ❷8–9
CROWN VETCH
PAPILIONACEAE

This shrub is normally grown for its foliage and tiny pealike flowers. A dense, bushy shrub, it carries fragrant bright yellow flowers in late winter and early spring, making it an excellent choice for year-round interest. Grow in light, moderately fertile, well-drained soil, and provide shelter from harsh winds.

32–60in / 32–60in

COTONEASTER HORIZONTALIS ❷5–7
ROSACEAE

Originally from West China, this species has spreading branches that eventually form a herringbone pattern. Its rounded leaves turn red in autumn, and are accompanied by pink-tinged white flowers in late spring and red fruit afterward. A good choice for maintaining interest throughout the year, this shrub thrives in moderately fertile, well-drained soil.

3ft / 5ft

COTONEASTER LACTEUS ❷7–9
COTONEASTER
ROSACEAE

This upright evergreen is ideal for north- or east-facing sites. Most cotoneasters have small leaves, but this one has large, leathery, oval foliage with gray undersides. White flowers in early summer are followed by showy clusters of bright red berries in autumn and winter. Thrives in most soils.

12ft / 12ft

CRINODENDRON HOOKERIANUM ❷9–10
CHILEAN LANTERN TREE
ELAEOCARPACEAE

An evergreen with sturdy, dense branches. Flower buds develop slowly in autumn and winter to provide a stunning red display of lantern-shaped flowers in late spring to early summer. It is quite fussy: the soil needs to be acid, and moist, yet well-drained. A warm, walled site will protect it in winter.

20ft / 15ft

---

 height and spread   ✳ feature of interest   ▮▮▮▮ season of interest   *SHRUBS* **C**

SHRUBS

CYTISUS BATTANDIERI ❷ 7–9
PINEAPPLE BROOM, MOROCCAN BROOM
PAPILIONACEAE

A choice broom for a high, south-facing wall. The yellow flowers, which have a strong pineapple scent in midsummer, are the main feature, but the silver-gray foliage is good too. Plants deteriorate after ten years or so because they do not shoot from old wood; prune lightly after flowering. Grow in fertile, well-drained soil.

15ft / 15ft

DESFONTAINIA SPINOSA ❷ 8–10
LOGANIACEAE

Cultivated for its hollylike spiky leaves and pendular flowers, this dense shrub originates from the Andes. Its ovate or oval, glossy, spiny leaves are joined by striking red flowers from midsummer to late autumn. In drier regions, it requires a cool, sheltered position. Grow in moist, lime-free, peaty soil.

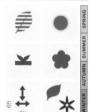

6ft / 6ft

DRIMYS WINTERI ❷ 8–10
WINTER'S BARK
WINTERACEAE

A conical, shrubby tree, this has long evergreen leaves, usually dark, with bluish-green undersides, and it produces clusters of scented, star-shaped white flowers in late spring. The bark is also aromatic. It needs shelter from cold winds, so a tall south- or west-facing wall is ideal. Grow in moist, but well-drained soil.

50ft / 30ft

ERIOBOTRYA JAPONICA ❷ 8–10
LOQUAT
ROSACEAE

A large shrub with a striking architectural shape. The leaves are very long and leathery, and their clearly visible veins add texture. In a hot summer, scented, hawthorn-type flowers may be produced, and sometimes pear-shaped orange fruits are borne. Needs a warm, sheltered wall and fertile, well-drained soil.

25ft / 25ft

ESCALLONIA 'IVEYI' ❷ 8–9
ESCALLONIACEAE

Originally found in areas of woodland and scrub, this upright shrub has attractive, glossy green leaves all year round, which can be bronze-tinted in winter. Fragrant white flowers are produced and carried from mid- to late summer in conical panicles. Grows well against a wall, in fertile, well-drained soil.

10ft / 10ft

EUONYMUS FORTUNEI 'SILVER QUEEN' ❷ 5–9
WINTER CREEPER
CELASTRACEAE

An easy evergreen that will flourish even in shade and in poor soils. When grown against a wall, the branching shoots produce aerial roots and eventually become self-clinging. There are other colorful variegated varieties, too, such as *E. f.* 'Emerald Gaiety' and 'Emerald 'n' Gold'. Grow in any well-drained soil.

8–20ft / 5ft

---

 leaf type   ● light preference   ♔ speed of growth   ❀ ease of growth

X FATSHEDERA LIZEI ❷ 8–10
TREE-IVY
ARALIACEAE

This loose, spreading shrub is a cross between Fatsia and Hedera and is prized for its foliage. Its large, palmate, lustrous green leaves are joined by small white flowers in autumn. A tough plant, it will shrug off pollution, shade, and salt spray. Excellent trained against a wall in fertile, moist, but well-drained soil.

FATSIA JAPONICA ❷ 8–10
JAPANESE ARALIA
ARALIACEAE

Originally from East Asia, this spreading, suckering, climbing shrub has thick stems and 7–11-lobed green leaves, and in autumn 5-petaled, creamy white flowers carried in umbels, followed by spherical black fruit. Another tough plant, it grows well in fertile, moist, but well-drained soil against a wall.

FORSYTHIA SUSPENSA ❷ 6–8
WEEPING FORSYTHIA
OLEACEAE

The bushy forsythias are well known, but this species and *F.* 'Beatrix Farrand' have long pliable shoots that make them ideal for training over arches or brightening up a north-facing wall. To prevent plants becoming leggy, prune lateral growth after flowering to within two buds of the old wood. Likes most soils.

FREMONTODENDRON CALIFORNICUM ❷ 8–10
CALIFORNIA FLANNEL BUSH
STERCULIACEAE

This tall semievergreen shrub produces a long-lasting display of round, yellow flowers. It is usual to grow them in the shelter of a south- or west-facing house wall. They dislike hard pruning and are short-lived. The stems shed fine hairs, which can irritate skin. Grow in poor to moderate, well-drained soil.

GARRYA ELLIPTICA ❷ 8–10
SILK TASSEL BUSH
GARRYACEAE

A wall shrub for interest in winter when it bears striking gray-green catkins. The leathery leaves are dark green. Not fussy about soil or position, and is a good choice in a garden subject to pollution or salt winds, although it looks better in a sheltered site. The variety *G. e.* 'James Roof' has extra-long tassels.

HIBISCUS SYRIACUS ❷ 5–9
MALVACEAE

Indigenous from China to India, this deciduous shrub has an erect nature. Its coarsely toothed diamond- or ovate-shaped leaves are topped by large trumpet-shaped dark pink flowers with yellow-anthered white stamens. These are produced from the leaf axils from late summer to mid-autumn. Hibiscus require a well-drained, neutral to alkaline soil to do well.

---

 height and spread　　✳ feature of interest　　◼◼◼◼ season of interest　　*SHRUBS* **C – H**

SHRUBS

HOHERIA LYALLII Z9–10

HOHERIA

MALVACEAE

A spreading shrub with striking deeply toothed and hairy leaves. When midsummer arrives, white flowers with purple anthers are produced. The species does best when sheltered from cold rasping winds, and therefore is ideal to grow near garden boundaries. Does best in a fertile, well-drained, neutral to acid soil.

22ft 22ft

ILEX AQUIFOLIUM 'ANGUSTIFOLIA' Z7–9

ENGLISH HOLLY

AQUIFOLIACEAE

The species is the common holly, a tolerant plant often used as hedging. In a small garden one of the many forms could be grown as a specimen. This form is a slow-growing, very erect tree. The leaves are very narrow and dark green, and the stems are purple. Likes moist, but well-drained, moderately fertile soil.

16ft 8ft

ITEA ILICIFOLIA Z7–9

ITEA, HOLLYLEAF SWEETSPIRE

ESCALLONIACEAE

This is an elegant wall shrub with unusual and eye-catching, catkinlike flowers with a delicate scent in late summer. The glossy, dark evergreen foliage is similar to that of a holly but requires shelter to keep it looking its best. A moist fertile soil is preferred. It requires very little pruning.

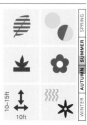

10–15ft 10ft

JASMINUM HUMILE 'REVOLUTUM' Z7–9

YELLOW JASMINE

OLEACEAE

Grown for its fragrant yellow flowers, this cultivar originates from India and Nepal. It has thick shoots and large leaves, and up to 12 large scented flowers measuring 1in (2.5cm) across. Grow in fertile, well-drained soil.

8ft 6ft

JASMINUM NUDIFLORUM Z6–9

WINTER JASMINE

OLEACEAE

A wall shrub rather than a true climber, this is a very hardy jasmine that thrives in all conditions. The yellow flowers, which are borne on bare stems, cheer up the winter garden. Although it can be allowed to sprawl, it is best tied in close to a wall and clipped hard after flowering. Grow in fertile, well-drained soil.

10ft 10ft

LAURUS NOBILIS Z8–10

SWEET BAY

LAURACEAE

A wonderfully aromatic conical tree whose leaves provide a popular flavoring in cooking. Glossy dark green leaves are enhanced in spring by clusters of greenish-yellow flowers. Female plants produce black berries in summer. Great against a sunny wall. Likes fertile, moist, but well-drained soil.

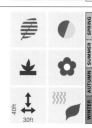

40ft 30ft

leaf type | light preference | speed of growth | ease of growth

LIGUSTRUM OVALIFOLIUM ❷6–8
CALIFORNIA PRIVET
OLEACEAE

From a genus of plants indigenous to Europe, North Africa, the Himalayas, parts of Asia, and Australia. Glossy green leaves are joined by panicles of white flowers which carry a disagreeable scent. Good for a shrub border or as specimen plants, they like most well-drained soils.

12ft / 12ft

MAGNOLIA GRANDIFLORA ❷7–9
BULL BAY, SOUTHERN MAGNOLIA
MAGNOLIACEAE

This magnolia can be grown as a wall shrub or freestanding tree. It bears enormous, fragrant white flowers from midsummer to early autumn; flowering starts on six-year-old plants. The leathery leaves are glossy green with red-brown undersides. Enrich sandy or poor soils with well-rotted organic matter.

20–60ft / 50ft

MELIANTHUS MAJOR ❷8–10
HONEY BUSH
MELIANTHACEAE

This tall, spreading shrub has gray-green to bright blue-gray pinnate leaves, usually carried near ground level. From late spring to midsummer, it produces crimson to deep red flowers on spiky racemes. Great for coastal gardens; protect from excessive winter cold. Likes moderately fertile, moist, but well-drained soil.

6–10ft / 3–10ft

MYRTUS COMMUNIS ❷8–9
COMMON MYRTLE
MYRTACEAE

An evergreen shrub with aromatic, glossy, dark green leaves, myrtle bears fragrant white flowers with prominent stamens in clusters in early to late summer. Small, dark purple berries sometimes follow in autumn. Plant against a south- or west-facing wall in colder gardens. Likes most soils.

10ft / 10ft

PHOTINIA X FRASERI 'RED ROBIN' ❷8–9
ROSACEAE

The bright red young foliage is the main feature of interest on this evergreen, but it sometimes produces small white flowers in spring. It is hardy, but the new foliage can be damaged by cold winds, so a south- or west-facing wall or fence will get the best out of it. Grow in fertile, moist, but well-drained soil.

15ft / 15ft

PHYGELIUS CAPENSIS ❷8–9
CAPE FIGWORT
SCROPHULARIACEAE

In mild areas against a warm wall the cape figwort is evergreen, but in colder sites it is treated like a herbaceous perennial and cut back to ground level each autumn. It will thrive in a sunny, sheltered spot and produce spikes of orange-red tubular flowers with yellow insides. Grow in fertile, moist soil.

4ft / 5ft

⬍ height and spread   ✳ feature of interest   ▭▭▭ season of interest   *SHRUBS* **H – P**

SHRUBS

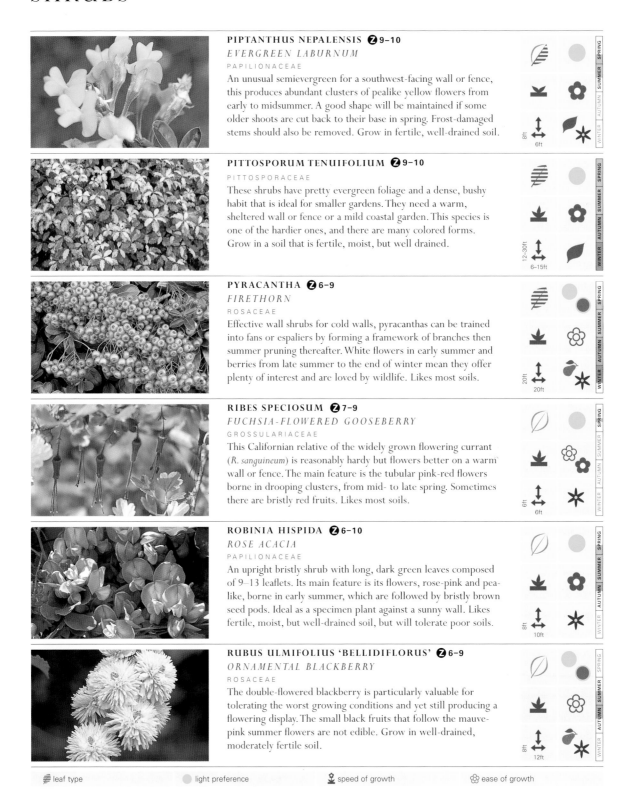

PIPTANTHUS NEPALENSIS ❷ 9–10
EVERGREEN LABURNUM
PAPILIONACEAE

An unusual semievergreen for a southwest-facing wall or fence, this produces abundant clusters of pealike yellow flowers from early to midsummer. A good shape will be maintained if some older shoots are cut back to their base in spring. Frost-damaged stems should also be removed. Grow in fertile, well-drained soil.

PITTOSPORUM TENUIFOLIUM ❷ 9–10
PITTOSPORACEAE

These shrubs have pretty evergreen foliage and a dense, bushy habit that is ideal for smaller gardens. They need a warm, sheltered wall or fence or a mild coastal garden. This species is one of the hardier ones, and there are many colored forms. Grow in a soil that is fertile, moist, but well drained.

PYRACANTHA ❷ 6–9
FIRETHORN
ROSACEAE

Effective wall shrubs for cold walls, pyracanthas can be trained into fans or espaliers by forming a framework of branches then summer pruning thereafter. White flowers in early summer and berries from late summer to the end of winter mean they offer plenty of interest and are loved by wildlife. Likes most soils.

RIBES SPECIOSUM ❷ 7–9
FUCHSIA-FLOWERED GOOSEBERRY
GROSSULARIACEAE

This Californian relative of the widely grown flowering currant (*R. sanguineum*) is reasonably hardy but flowers better on a warm wall or fence. The main feature is the tubular pink-red flowers borne in drooping clusters, from mid- to late spring. Sometimes there are bristly red fruits. Likes most soils.

ROBINIA HISPIDA ❷ 6–10
ROSE ACACIA
PAPILIONACEAE

An upright bristly shrub with long, dark green leaves composed of 9–13 leaflets. Its main feature is its flowers, rose-pink and pea-like, borne in early summer, which are followed by bristly brown seed pods. Ideal as a specimen plant against a sunny wall. Likes fertile, moist, but well-drained soil, but will tolerate poor soils.

RUBUS ULMIFOLIUS 'BELLIDIFLORUS' ❷ 6–9
ORNAMENTAL BLACKBERRY
ROSACEAE

The double-flowered blackberry is particularly valuable for tolerating the worst growing conditions and yet still producing a flowering display. The small black fruits that follow the mauve-pink summer flowers are not edible. Grow in well-drained, moderately fertile soil.

🪶 leaf type   ⬤ light preference   🌱 speed of growth   ⚜ ease of growth

SOLANUM CRISPUM 'GLASNEVIN' ❷ 9–10
CHILEAN POTATO TREE
SOLANACEAE

One of the best flowering wall shrubs, this particular variety, which was formerly known as *S. c.* 'Autumnale', is hardier than the species and flowers longer. Give it a sunny spot against a south- or west-facing fence or wall if you have one. Tie it into horizontal wires to prevent it sprawling. Grow in any soil. Evergreen or semievergreen.

20ft / 15ft

SOPHORA TETRAPTERA ❷ 9–10
KOWHAI
PAPILIONACEAE

A spreading evergreen tree or shrub with pinnate leaves consisting of up to 20 pairs of dark green leaflets. Grown for its elegant racemes of golden yellow flowers, which are produced in late spring. Great for a sunny wall. This species requires moderately fertile, well-drained soil.

30ft / 15ft

STAPHYLEA COLCHICA ❷ 6–9
BLADDERNUT
STAPHYLEACEAE

Part of a genus of shrubs and small trees found in woodland and thickets in temperate northern regions. Upright nature with pinnate, glossy green leaves, with ovate leaflets in late spring, it produces bell-shaped scented white flowers, followed by greenish fruit. Requires moist, but well-drained soil.

11ft / 11ft

TEUCRIUM FRUTICANS ❷ 8–9
SHRUBBY GERMANDER
LAMIACEAE

A great all-rounder that will bring interest to your garden throughout the seasons. Its ovate to lance-shaped gray-green leaves are woolly-white underneath. Complemented in summer by pale blue flowers with prominent stamens, borne in terminal racemes. Requires well-drained, neutral to alkaline soil.

24–39ft / 12ft

VINCA MINOR ❷ 4–9
CREEPING PERIWINKLE
APOCYNACEAE

This evergreen shrub and its varieties are useful long-term container subjects. It is worth buying a named variety for extra color, either in terms of variegated foliage or of large or more profuse flowers. For maximum flowers provide a site in full sun. Likes almost any type of soil.

4–8in / 3ft

VITEX AGNUS-CASTUS ❷ 6–9
CHASTE TREE
VERBENACEAE

This deciduous shrub has attractive dark green foliage divided into leaflets. The flowers, which resemble those of lilac, are scented, violet-blue, and appear in early autumn. It will perform best if fan-trained against a south- or west-facing wall, particularly in colder areas. Grow in any well-drained soil.

6–25ft / 6–25ft

---

 height and spread   feature of interest   season of interest   *SHRUBS* **P – V**

CLIMBERS

ACTINIDIA DELICIOSA ❷7–9
CHINESE GOOSEBERRY
ACTINIDIACEAE

This species is a distinctly vigorous plant with chunky shoots and heart-shaped, mid-green leaves. Creamy white to yellow flowers are produced in early summer in clusters of 2 or 3. The female plants produce bristly, greenish-brown fruit. Requires fertile, well-drained soil.

30ft ↕ 30ft

ACTINIDIA KOLOMIKTA ❷5–8
ACTINIDIA
ACTINIDIACEAE

This is a valuable ornamental foliage plant for covering a sunny, sheltered wall or fence. Once the plant is a couple of years old, the heart-shaped leaves start pale green, then acquire white and pink variations, before turning an attractive red in autumn. Cats are attracted to the plant. Grow in fertile, well-drained soil.

15ft ↕ 15ft

AKEBIA QUINATA ❷5–9
CHOCOLATE VINE
LARDIZABALACEAE

A semievergreen, with 5 leaflets to each leaf and chocolate-scented, purple-maroon flowers, this is an attractive, informal plant for rambling through host plants or covering walls or fences. It is useful because there are few flowering climbers that tolerate cool, shady walls. Grow in moist, but well-drained soil. Restrain growth by pruning.

30ft ↕ 30ft

AMPELOPSIS BREVIPEDUNCULATA ❷5–8
VITACEAE

A vigorous climber from North East Asia, grown for its foliage and its fruit. Its palmately 3- to 5-lobed dark green leaves turn most attractive shades of red and yellow in autumn. Axillary cymes of small green flowers are produced in summer, followed by pinkish-purple spherical fruit, which later turn blue. Will do well in any moist, well-drained, and fertile soil. Invasive plant.

15ft ↕ 15ft

AMPELOPSIS BREVIPEDUNCULATA 'ELEGANS' ❷5–8
PORCELAIN BERRY
VITACEAE

This cultivar is a less vigorous plant. Its leaves are an attractive dark green, mottled white and pink. Small green flowers are produced in summer, bettered by its fruit, which start off pinkish-purple and turn clear blue. Will do well in any moist, well-drained, and fertile soil. Invasive plant.

15ft ↕ 15ft

ARISTOLOCHIA MACROPHYLLA ❷5–8
DUTCHMAN'S PIPE
ARISTOLOCHIACEAE

Great for screening unattractive sights, this genus gets its common name because of the shape of its flowers. Its single, rounded mid-green flowers have an S-shaped calyx with an inflated base, resembling the shape of a Dutch pipe. Grow in well-drained, humus-rich, fertile soil.

25–30ft ↕ 25–30ft

≣ leaf type   ● light preference   ⚘ speed of growth   ⊛ ease of growth

BERBERIDOPSIS CORALLINA ❷8–9
CORAL PLANT
FLACOURTIACEAE

A choice South American climbing shrub, this is hardy but needs a sheltered spot to protect it from drying winds. The flowers are sometimes followed by red berries. An arch or pergola would display the flowers well. Mulch and protect the base in winter in cold gardens. Needs lime-free soil.

15ft / 15ft

CAMPSIS GRANDIFLORA ❷7–9
CHINESE TRUMPET CREEPER
BIGNONIACEAE

This climber has opposite, pinnate leaves composed of 7–9 ovate, coarsely toothed leaflets. From late summer to autumn, it bears pendent, terminal panicles of open funnel-shaped, dark orange to red flowers. Needs to be trained against a wall, fence, or pillar. Grow in fertile, moist, but well-drained soil.

30ft / 30ft

CAMPSIS RADICANS ❷5–9
COMMON TRUMPET CREEPER
BIGNONIACEAE

A rapid grower whose dark green leaves are composed of 7–11 toothed, ovate leaflets. It will bear terminal cymes of slender, tubular-trumpet-shaped, orange to red flowers from late summer to autumn. Grow in fertile, moist, but well-drained soil.

30ft / 30ft

CAMPSIS X TAGLIABUANA 'MADAME GALEN' ❷5–9
TRUMPET CREEPER
BIGNONIACEAE

This vigorous climber has pinnate, dark green leaves with 7–11 ovate leaflets. Its trumpet-shaped, orange-red flowers are carried from summer to autumn. Takes time to settle down and flower. Will do best in fertile, moist, but well-drained soil.

30ft / 30ft

CELASTRUS ORBICULATUS ❷4–8
ORIENTAL BITTERSWEET
CELASTRACEAE

This variety is a vigorous, woody climber with elliptic to rounded finely toothed leaves, which turn a wonderful yellow with the arrival of autumn. Small green flowers appear in summer, followed by beadlike yellow fruit which carry pinky-red seeds. Will need strong support, and a well-drained soil. Can be invasive and weedy.

40–50ft / 40ft

CELASTRUS SCANDENS ❷3–8
AMERICAN BITTERSWEET
CELASTRACEAE

Another woody, deciduous climber with oval to ovate, mid-green leaves. It produces small, yellow-green flowers in summer, which are followed by clusters of orange-yellow fruit, which, like all cultivars of this genus, have attractive seeds. Will need strong support, and a well-drained soil.

30ft / 30ft

---

 height and spread   ✻ feature of interest   ▮▮▮▮ season of interest   *CLIMBERS* **A – C**

CLIMBERS

CLEMATIS ALPINA 'FRANCES RIVIS' ❷ 6–9
ALPINE CLEMATIS
RANUNCULACEAE

Dainty in appearance yet tough enough to survive shade and cold, alpinas are easy clematis for any garden. This variety is superior to the species as there are lots of larger flowers of a clear, pale blue. Grow in fertile, humus-rich, well-drained soil.

6–10ft
5ft

CLEMATIS ARMANDII 'APPLE BLOSSOM' ❷ 7–9
EVERGREEN CLEMATIS
RANUNCULACEAE

A warm sheltered spot is essential, preferably where there is plenty of room for it to roam. The glossy foliage is valuable year-round cover. For the best flowers get *C. a.* 'Apple Blossom' for its pink buds and white perfumed flowers. Grow in fertile, humus-rich, well-drained soil.

10–15ft
6–10ft

CLEMATIS CAMPANIFLORA ❷ 7–9
RANUNCULACEAE

This species is related to *C. viticella* but is more vigorous. Masses of little bell flowers in white or pale blue are produced in midsummer. Grow it up trees or large shrubs, or combine it with a dark-leaved climber. Grow in fertile, well-drained soil.

10–15ft
10ft

CLEMATIS CIRRHOSA VAR. BALEARICA ❷ 7–9
WINTER-FLOWERING CLEMATIS
RANUNCULACEAE

A winter-interest clematis for a warm, sheltered site. The belllike flowers are cream colored with red-brown spots. The evergreen foliage is finely divided, almost fernlike, and turns from green in summer to bronze in autumn and winter. Will need fertile, humus-rich, well-drained soil to do well.

8–10ft
6ft

CLEMATIS X DURANDII ❷ 6–9
RANUNCULACEAE

This is a nonclinging clematis that requires staking. Good for sustaining interest in the vertical garden, as its single, saucerlike indigo-blue flowers are produced late in the season. Will need fertile, humus-rich, well-drained soil to do well.

3–6ft
3ft

CLEMATIS X ERIOSTEMON ❷ 4–9
RANUNCULACEAE

This woody-based climber bears an abundance of small, solitary bell-shaped flowers with deep indigo sepals and creamy yellow anthers. Of garden origin, it will need fertile, humus-rich, well-drained soil to do well, and will require strong support.

9ft
3ft

 leaf type    light preference   🌱 speed of growth   🏵 ease of growth

CLEMATIS FLAMMULA ❷ 7–9
FRAGRANT VIRGIN'S BOWER
RANUNCULACEAE

In summer large clusters of small flowers cover this tall plant. The flowers have a strong sweet scent that is best appreciated in a warm sheltered spot. This vigorous clematis needs regular pruning to keep it attractive. It will need fertile, humus-rich, well-drained soil to do well.

CLEMATIS FLORIDA 'BICOLOR' ❷ 6–9
PASSION FLOWER CLEMATIS
RANUNCULACEAE

A semievergreen climber, prized for its large, single, white-creamy flowers which are sported in late spring to early summer. It will need fertile, humus-rich, well-drained soil to do well, and will require strong support.

CLEMATIS X JOUINIANA 'PRAECOX' ❷ 4–9
RANUNCULACEAE

A nonclinging clematis with masses of pale mauve flowers that fade through pink to white. They appear in large clusters from late summer into autumn. The form 'Praecox' flowers slightly earlier, during mid- and late summer. The deciduous leaves are large and rather coarse, and turn yellow in autumn. Can be grown up walls but very good for obelisks. It needs tying in.

CLEMATIS MACROPETALA 'MAIDWELL HALL' ❷ 6–9
RANUNCULACEAE

The macropetala varieties have slightly fuller flowers than the alpinas but are otherwise the same, sharing the same tough constitution for cold or shaded places. There are many blue varieties, but *C. m.* 'Maidwell Hall' is a particularly deep blue. Grow in fertile, humus-rich, well-drained soil.

CLEMATIS MONTANA F. GRANDIFLORA ❷ 6–9
RANUNCULACEAE

As its name suggests, this is a large clematis both in stature and flower size. The dark green foliage makes an excellent foil for the abundance of white flowers. An impressive flowering climber for a large north wall. Grow in a fertile, humus-rich, well-drained soil.

CLEMATIS MONTANA VAR. RUBENS ❷ 6–9
RANUNCULACEAE

A group of clematis with small pink flowers, the shade of pink varying with the form of the plant. The best ones are a mauve-pink with contrasting stamens. The young stems and leaf stalks are a red-purple, and the young foliage is tinged with purple. Grow in fertile, humus-rich, well-drained soil.

↕ height and spread   ✳ feature of interest   ▨▨▨ season of interest   *CLIMBERS* **C**

CLIMBERS

CLEMATIS MONTANA VAR. SERICEA ❷ 6–9

RANUNCULACEAE

A very attractive clematis with masses of pale pink flowers in the spring. It has an attractive bronze-colored foliage and golden hairs on the buds, but no perfume. It grows in the same situation as any other montana type. Sometimes incorrectly labeled as *C. chrysocoma* and it is also listed as *C. spooneri*.

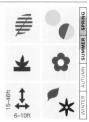

15–46ft / 6–10ft

CLEMATIS ORIENTALIS ❷ 6–9

RANUNCULACEAE

A very attractive, small-flowered clematis for late summer and into autumn. The flowers are yellow with four incurving petals that hang like a partly-peeled orange. The foliage is also very attractive, being finely cut. Once established, the growth is vigorous and although it grows high it is also quite bushy. Its hybrid 'Bill MacKenzie' is one of the best forms.

22ft / 6–10ft

CLEMATIS REHDERIANA ❷ 6–9

RANUNCULACEAE

A vigorous clematis originally from western China, grown for its wonderful yellow flowers. Produced late in the season, they are tubular and cowslip-scented, with creamy yellow anthers. Grow in fertile, humus-rich, well-drained soil, ensuring that the roots and base of the plant remain in shade.

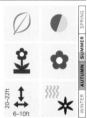

20–22ft / 6–10ft

CLEMATIS TANGUTICA ❷ 6–9

RUSSIAN VIRGIN'S BOWER

RANUNCULACEAE

The abundant, single, bell-shaped flowers of this clematis are produced from midsummer to late autumn. These are followed by attractive fluffy seed heads. Grow in fertile, humus-rich, well-drained soil, ensuring that the roots and base of the plant remain in shade.

15–20ft / 6–10ft

CLEMATIS TEXENSIS ❷ 4–9

SCARLET CLEMATIS

RANUNCULACEAE

Another late-flowering climber, this clematis produces solitary, bell-shaped, pinky-red flowers toward the end of summer. Grow in fertile, humus-rich, well-drained soil, ensuring that the roots and base of the plant remain in shade.

6–15ft / 1–2ft

CLEMATIS VITALBA ❷ 6–9

OLD MAN'S BEARD, TRAVELLER'S JOY

RANUNCULACEAE

This clematis has very small flowers that appear in frothy heads. It is very vigorous and can become rampant in the right situation. It is a plant for the wild garden and works best growing through trees or over fences, but is best avoided on walls and more ornamental situations. It flowers in late summer.

25–30ft / 10ft

🌿 leaf type   ⬤ light preference   🌱 speed of growth   ✿ ease of growth

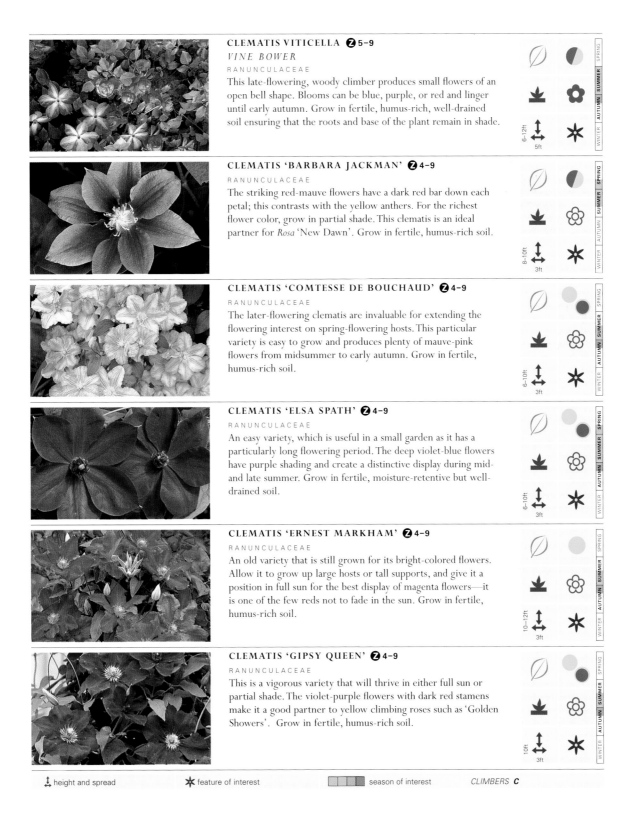

CLEMATIS VITICELLA ❷ 5–9
VINE BOWER
RANUNCULACEAE

This late-flowering, woody climber produces small flowers of an open bell shape. Blooms can be blue, purple, or red and linger until early autumn. Grow in fertile, humus-rich, well-drained soil ensuring that the roots and base of the plant remain in shade.

6–12ft
5ft

CLEMATIS 'BARBARA JACKMAN' ❷ 4–9
RANUNCULACEAE

The striking red-mauve flowers have a dark red bar down each petal; this contrasts with the yellow anthers. For the richest flower color, grow in partial shade. This clematis is an ideal partner for *Rosa* 'New Dawn'. Grow in fertile, humus-rich soil.

8–10ft
3ft

CLEMATIS 'COMTESSE DE BOUCHAUD' ❷ 4–9
RANUNCULACEAE

The later-flowering clematis are invaluable for extending the flowering interest on spring-flowering hosts. This particular variety is easy to grow and produces plenty of mauve-pink flowers from midsummer to early autumn. Grow in fertile, humus-rich soil.

6–10ft
3ft

CLEMATIS 'ELSA SPATH' ❷ 4–9
RANUNCULACEAE

An easy variety, which is useful in a small garden as it has a particularly long flowering period. The deep violet-blue flowers have purple shading and create a distinctive display during mid- and late summer. Grow in fertile, moisture-retentive but well-drained soil.

6–10ft
3ft

CLEMATIS 'ERNEST MARKHAM' ❷ 4–9
RANUNCULACEAE

An old variety that is still grown for its bright-colored flowers. Allow it to grow up large hosts or tall supports, and give it a position in full sun for the best display of magenta flowers—it is one of the few reds not to fade in the sun. Grow in fertile, humus-rich soil.

10–12ft
3ft

CLEMATIS 'GIPSY QUEEN' ❷ 4–9
RANUNCULACEAE

This is a vigorous variety that will thrive in either full sun or partial shade. The violet-purple flowers with dark red stamens make it a good partner to yellow climbing roses such as 'Golden Showers'. Grow in fertile, humus-rich soil.

10ft
3ft

⬍ height and spread   ✳ feature of interest   ▢▢▢ season of interest   *CLIMBERS* **C**

CLIMBERS

CLEMATIS 'HAGLEY HYBRID' ❷ 4–9
RANUNCULACEAE
This fairly short variety is easy to manage and is reliable.
Grow over shrubs, including shrub roses, or other supports.
The flowers are pink with brown stamens; for the best color keep
them out of direct sunlight. Grow in fertile soil.

CLEMATIS 'JACKMANII SUPERBA' ❷ 4–9
RANUNCULACEAE
A larger-flowered version of the well-known *C. jackmanii* with
the characteristic velvet purple flowers. Pair it with deep yellow
flowers such as *Rosa* 'Maigold' for a good color contrast. Grow in
fertile, humus-rich soil.

CLEMATIS 'MARIE BOISSELOT' ❷ 4–9
RANUNCULACEAE
This vigorous grower combines well with ivies or honeysuckles.
The large, pure white flowers, which look stunning against a dark
green foil, open from pink buds and last well. It can be used as a
cut flower. Grow in fertile, humus-rich soil.

CLEMATIS 'MISS BATEMAN' ❷ 4–9
RANUNCULACEAE
A compact clematis which bears its flowers early in the year.
The single blooms are large and plentiful, rounded and white
with red anthers. Grow in fertile, humus-rich soil.

CLEMATIS 'MRS CHOLMONDELEY' ❷ 4–9
RANUNCULACEAE
The large flowers are a lovely lavender blue, with contrasting
brown anthers. For the best color grow in partial shade. A long-
flowering variety, which combines well with pink roses, such as
R. 'Bantry Bay'. Grow in a soil that is fertile and humus-rich.
One of the longest flowering varieties.

CLEMATIS 'NELLY MOSER' ❷ 4–9
RANUNCULACEAE
This well-known variety bears large flowers of pale pink marked
with a bright pink band on each petal. It is easy to grow and
ideal for brightening up shady or north-facing aspects. Grow in
a soil that is fertile and humus-rich.

≋ leaf type   ● light preference   ⚓ speed of growth   ❀ ease of growth

CLEMATIS 'NIOBE' ❷ 4–9

RANUNCULACEAE

Deep velvet-red flowers with yellow anthers are borne from late spring to early autumn. An ideal partner for a Japanese honeysuckle or a medium-sized shrub. Grow in a soil that is fertile and humus-rich.

6–10ft / 3ft

CLEMATIS 'PERLE D'AZUR' ❷ 4–9

RANUNCULACEAE

A rather vigorous clematis, prized for the light blue color of its flowers. Use the color in combination with other climbers such as pink-flowered roses or a *C. viticella*, which would flower at the same time. Grow in a soil that is fertile and humus-rich.

10ft / 3ft

CLEMATIS 'PROTEUS' ❷ 4–9

RANUNCULACEAE

Although an old variety, this is still popular for its large mauve-pink blooms, which can be double, semidouble, or single. It is best grown in a sheltered position such as through a medium-sized shrub, in fertile, humus-rich soil. A sunny position is needed to avoid green flowers.

8–10ft / 3ft

CLEMATIS 'THE PRESIDENT' ❷ 4–9

RANUNCULACEAE

A strong grower that will thrive almost anywhere. It flowers reliably from late spring to early autumn, and the blooms are large and a rich purple with silver undersides. Grow in a soil that is fertile and humus-rich.

6–10ft / 3ft

CLEMATIS 'VILLE DE LYON' ❷ 4–9

RANUNCULACEAE

The blooms are a bright cherry red with contrasting yellow anthers. Combine it with another strong color, such as a yellow-leaved ivy. Hard pruning can keep it at 10ft (3m), but it will otherwise grow much taller. Grow in a soil that is fertile and humus-rich.

6–10ft / 3ft

CLEMATIS 'VYVYAN PENNELL' ❷ 4–9

OLD MAN'S BEARD, TRAVELLER'S JOY

RANUNCULACEAE

There are beautiful double flowers initially, followed by a second flush of single blooms. The flower color is a mixture of blue, violet, and purple. Grow where the flowers get the sun to prevent the outer petals turning green. Plant deeply in fertile soil because this variety is prone to clematis wilt.

6–10ft / 3ft

↨ height and spread   ✳ feature of interest   ▭▭▭▭ season of interest   *CLIMBERS* **C**

CLIMBERS

CLEMATIS 'WILLIAM KENNETT' **Z** 6–9
RANUNCULACEAE

This clematis is an early flowerer, producing single, lavender-blue flowers with dark red anthers at the beginning of summer. The sepal of each flower fades as the flower grows. Grow in fertile, humus-rich, well-drained soil.

6–10ft
3ft

COBAEA SCANDENS **Z** 10–11
CUP-AND-SAUCER PLANT
POLEMONIACEAE

An annual climber that has leaves with 4 elliptic, green leaflets, 2 basal stipules, and a large branched tendril with tiny hooks. Summer brings fragrant creamy-green flowers which turn purple with age. Grow in fertile, humus-rich, well-drained soil in a sheltered site. Perfect for growing against a wall in warm areas.

30–70ft
30ft

CODONOPSIS CONVOLVULACEA **Z** 7–9
CLIMBING HAREBELL
CAMPANULACEAE

This is a hardy perennial but it can be treated like an annual—it often flowers the first year from seed or tubers and dies down in winter. Grow it where you can look up into the flowers— for example, in a raised pot with small supports. Other species are available but not all climb. Grow in light, fertile soil.

6ft
6ft

CONVOLVULUS SABATIUS **Z** 8–9
CONVOLVULACEAE

A trailing perennial originally from parts of Spain, Italy, and North Africa. From summer to early autumn the plant bears a profusion of trumpet-shaped blue flowers. Needs protection in winter. Likes a soil that is poor to moderately fertile, well-drained, and gritty.

6in
20in

CUCURBITA PEPO **Z** 3–11
ORNAMENTAL GOURD
CUCURBITACEAE

An arch, pergola, or walkway bedecked with hanging gourds is a real talking point for autumn, and it saves on ground space too. Use trailing varieties and make sure the support is strong. Allow the fruit to mature on the vine, then cut and dry thoroughly.

3–30ft
3ft

ECCREMOCARPUS SCABER **Z** 10–11
CHILEAN GLORY FLOWER
BIGNONIACEAE

The tubular orange flowers add rich summer color when grown in tandem with shrubs, hedge, or other climbers. Named varieties have extended the color range to include red, pink, and yellow. Grow as a half-hardy annual; it will overwinter in mild areas and sometimes self-seeds. Plant in fertile, well-drained soil.

10–15ft
10ft

≣ leaf type   ● light preference   ⚇ speed of growth   ⚘ ease of growth

FALLOPIA BALDSCHUANICA ⓩ5–9
RUSSIAN VINE
POLYGONACEAE

This plant is here as a warning rather than as a recommendation because it is extremely invasive. Introduce it only for large buildings or tall trees. It is attractive when covered in clusters of small white flowers in late summer. It was previously known as *Polygonum baldschuanicum*. Grow in poor to moderate soil.

HEDERA CANARIENSIS ⓩ6–10
CANARY ISLAND IVY
ARALIACEAE

The large, glossy leaves of this plant are shaped like arrowheads and make rapid, self-clinging cover. Less hardy than the English ivy (*H. helix*), the leaves may die in a hard winter, though they will often regrow. The stems are an attractive red-green.

HEDERA CANARIENSIS 'GLOIRE DE MARENGO' ⓩ7–10
CANARY ISLAND IVY
ARALIACEAE

The fastest growing variegated ivy, this makes an ideal cover for a house wall. It is more decorative than the species, having silver-gray splashes on the cream-edged leaves and deep red stems. It is hardy, but leaves are often lost in cold winters. This variety is sometimes sold as *H. canariensis* 'Variegata'. Tolerates most soils.

HEDERA COLCHICA ⓩ5–10
PERSIAN IVY
ARALIACEAE

This is a tolerant ivy, ideal for tough conditions. The dark green foliage consists of large, heart-shaped leaves with a leathery texture. It does not cling by itself at first, but will scramble up supports once started off. All the *H. colchica* ivies emit a resiny odor when crushed. Tolerates most soils.

HEDERA COLCHICA 'SULPHUR HEART' ⓩ5–10
BULLOCK'S HEART IVY, PERSIAN IVY
ARALIACEAE

This variety, with its large, light green leaves splashed with yellow, is sometimes called *H. c.* 'Paddy's Pride'. A vigorous grower, it makes very dense cover for walls or fences. It works well with *Jasminum nudiflorum* as a winter color combination. Tolerates most soils.

HEDERA HELIX ⓩ5–10
ENGLISH IVY
ARALIACEAE

This species is a perfect choice for a less formal vertical garden. It is a vigorous self-clinging climber, or could also be used as a trailing perennial to cover walls. Leaves are 3–5-lobed, ovate to triangular, and are a rich glossy green. Tolerates most soils.

---

 height and spread   ✱ feature of interest   ▭▭▭ season of interest   *CLIMBERS* **C – H**

CLIMBERS

HEDERA HELIX 'ADAM' ❷5–10

ARALIACEAE

Slightly less hardy than a typical *H. helix* variety, this branching ivy can lose its foliage in hard winters but it soon recovers. The leaves are small and pale green, and age to gray; each has a cream-white edge. In cold weather the edges turn pink.

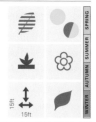

HEDERA HELIX 'BUTTERCUP' ❷5–10

ARALIACEAE

A pretty ivy that combines well with flowering climbers such as blue or purple clematis. To get the bright yellow coloration, a sunny position is essential. Even in sun, some leaves will be a proper yellow and others a yellow-green. In shade the foliage will be a paler yellow. Tolerates most soils.

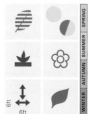

HEDERA HELIX 'GLACIER' ❷5–10

ARALIACEAE

The coloration of this popular variety makes it an ideal backdrop to cool color schemes. The small leaves, gray-green splashed with silver, have narrow cream edges. It is often used in container planting and as a houseplant, although it is fairly hardy. Tolerates most soils.

HEDERA HELIX 'GREEN RIPPLE' ❷5–10

ARALIACEAE

An invaluable ivy with bright green foliage and green-purple stems. Each leaf has a pronounced leaf edge, which gives the whole plant an interesting texture and shape. It is versatile and can be used for growing up walls or for cascading down from wall planters.

HEDERA HELIX 'ORO DI BOGLIASCO' ❷5–10

ARALIACEAE

A colorful variety, also called *H. h.* 'Goldheart', this ivy has green leaves, which are splashed with pale yellow, and young red-pink shoots. It produces the best variegation when grown vertically rather than on the ground, but do cut out any reverted shoots. Tolerates most soils.

HEDERA HELIX 'PARSLEY CRESTED' ❷5–10

ARALIACEAE

The light, fresh green leaves of this ivy, which is often sold as *H. h.* 'Cristata', have crimped edges. The stems are green-purple. It branches well and trails readily, so it can be used in wall planters or on walls. There is some reddening of the foliage in winter. Tolerates most soils.

≣ leaf type	● light preference	♠ speed of growth	✿ ease of growth

HEDERA HELIX 'SAGITTIFOLIA' ❷ 5–10

ARALIACEAE

The true variety is a dark green ivy with a vining habit, suitable for growing up walls and trees. Each leaf has the shape of a "bird's foot". It should not be confused with the ivy sold as a houseplant that is often given this name. *H. h.* 'Sagittifolia Variegata,' shown here, is a less vigorous form, useful for containers. Tolerates most soils.

HEDERA HIBERNICA ❷ 6–10

IRISH IVY

ARALIACEAE

This vigorous climbing ivy is useful for quickly covering eyesores. The large, heart-shaped leaves are a rather dull green with gray-green veins. It makes an unobtrusive backdrop to more colorful plantings, although there is a variegated form with yellow markings. Tolerates most soils.

HOLBOELLIA CORIACEA ❷ 10–11

HOLBOELLIA

LARDIZABALACEAE

The main feature of interest of this Chinese evergreen is the glossy, dark green foliage. It is slightly tender but will grow in shade although sun is needed to fruit. The sausage-shaped, purple fruits are rarely produced unless it has been a hot summer and the plant is grown in sun. Likes most soils.

HUMULUS LUPULUS 'AUREUS' ❷ 4–8

GOLDEN HOP

CANNABACEAE

The quick-covering, lush golden foliage is attractive when it is grown over a blue or black trellis or in combination with purple clematis. Growth becomes slightly untidy but will die down by winter, as this plant is a herbaceous perennial. There are attractive fruits—hops. Grow in moist, well-drained soils.

HYDRANGEA ANOMALA SUBSP. PETIOLARIS ❷ 4–9

CLIMBING HYDRANGEA

HYDRANGEACEAE

Attractive rounded leaves, a froth of creamy flower bracts, and peeling, coppery stems are all good features. This is one of those plants that improve with age; it eventually becomes selfclinging but needs tying in at first. Suitable for 10ft (3m) walls, despite its height, and invaluable for a north wall. Avoid chalky soils.

IPOMOEA LOBATA ❷ 10–11

SPANISH FLAG

CONVOLVULACEAE

This exotic-looking climber with its fiery flowers comes from South America. A perennial, grown as a half-hardy annual, use it for quick cover on a sheltered fence or wall. Its flowers provide color well into autumn. You may find it sold as *Mina lobata* or *I. versicolor*. Grow in moderately fertile, well-drained soil.

---

 height and spread   ✳ feature of interest    season of interest   *CLIMBERS* **H – I**

CLIMBERS

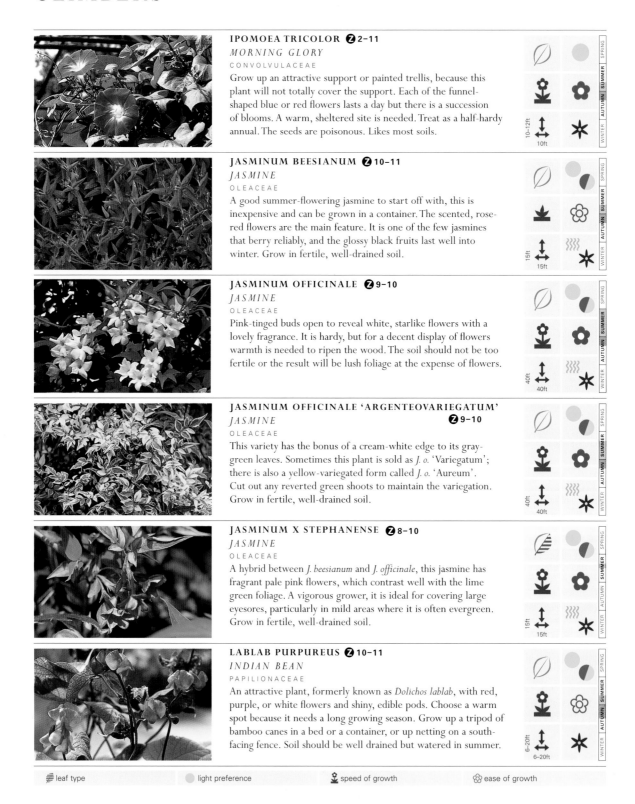

IPOMOEA TRICOLOR ⓩ 2-11
MORNING GLORY
CONVOLVULACEAE

Grow up an attractive support or painted trellis, because this plant will not totally cover the support. Each of the funnel-shaped blue or red flowers lasts a day but there is a succession of blooms. A warm, sheltered site is needed. Treat as a half-hardy annual. The seeds are poisonous. Likes most soils.

JASMINUM BEESIANUM ⓩ 10-11
JASMINE
OLEACEAE

A good summer-flowering jasmine to start off with, this is inexpensive and can be grown in a container. The scented, rose-red flowers are the main feature. It is one of the few jasmines that berry reliably, and the glossy black fruits last well into winter. Grow in fertile, well-drained soil.

JASMINUM OFFICINALE ⓩ 9-10
JASMINE
OLEACEAE

Pink-tinged buds open to reveal white, starlike flowers with a lovely fragrance. It is hardy, but for a decent display of flowers warmth is needed to ripen the wood. The soil should not be too fertile or the result will be lush foliage at the expense of flowers.

JASMINUM OFFICINALE 'ARGENTEOVARIEGATUM'
JASMINE   ⓩ 9-10
OLEACEAE

This variety has the bonus of a cream-white edge to its gray-green leaves. Sometimes this plant is sold as *J. o.* 'Variegatum'; there is also a yellow-variegated form called *J. o.* 'Aureum'. Cut out any reverted green shoots to maintain the variegation. Grow in fertile, well-drained soil.

JASMINUM X STEPHANENSE ⓩ 8-10
JASMINE
OLEACEAE

A hybrid between *J. beesianum* and *J. officinale*, this jasmine has fragrant pale pink flowers, which contrast well with the lime green foliage. A vigorous grower, it is ideal for covering large eyesores, particularly in mild areas where it is often evergreen. Grow in fertile, well-drained soil.

LABLAB PURPUREUS ⓩ 10-11
INDIAN BEAN
PAPILIONACEAE

An attractive plant, formerly known as *Dolichos lablab*, with red, purple, or white flowers and shiny, edible pods. Choose a warm spot because it needs a long growing season. Grow up a tripod of bamboo canes in a bed or a container, or up netting on a south-facing fence. Soil should be well drained but watered in summer.

🌿 leaf type   ● light preference   🌱 speed of growth   ✿ ease of growth

LATHYRUS LATIFOLIUS ❷ 5–9

EVERLASTING PEA

PAPILIONACEAE

This attractive species has winged stems and blue-green leaves consisting of single pairs of oblong leaflets. Between summer and early autumn, the plant will produce racemes of pinky-purple flowers. Grow in fertile, well-drained, humus-rich soil.

6ft / 6ft

LATHYRUS ODORATUS ❷ 2–11

SWEET PEA

PAPILIONACEAE

Few varieties combine beautiful flowers with the delicious scent, so decide what is most important to you before choosing a variety. Where ground space is at a premium, grow sweet peas up a tripod or up netting over a sunny fence rather than the traditional row of bamboo canes. Grow in fertile, well-drained soil.

6–8ft / 6–8ft

LATHYRUS SATIVUS ❷ 2–11

CHICKLING PEA

PAPILIONACEAE

This scrambling annual climber is indigenous to Central and South Europe, North Africa, and parts of Asia. Its winged stems and mid-green leaves divided into pairs of pointed leaflets are joined by pretty veined blue flowers that eventually fade to white. Grow in fertile, well-drained, humus-rich soil.

3ft / 18in

LONICERA X BROWNII 'DROPMORE SCARLET' ❷ 4–9

SCARLET TRUMPET HONEYSUCKLE

CAPRIFOLIACEAE

Unusually, this honeysuckle is grown for its flower color (there is no fragrance). Clusters of vivid scarlet flowers are borne from early summer to autumn. Grow in a shady spot to reduce the chances of aphid attack. Grow in fertile, humus-rich, moist, but well-drained soil.

12ft / 12ft

LONICERA CAPRIFOLIUM ❷ 6–9

ITALIAN HONEYSUCKLE

CAPRIFOLIACEAE

This woody, twining climber has paired, gray-green leaves, but is grown for its flowers and berries. In summer, whorls of lipped, tubular, yellowy flowers are produced, followed by orange-red berries. Grow in fertile, humus-rich, moist, but well-drained soil.

20ft / 20ft

LONICERA ETRUSCA 'SUPERBA' ❷ 7–9

ETRUSCAN HONEYSUCKLE

CAPRIFOLIACEAE

The large trusses of scented flowers are cream-yellow, aging to orange, and flowering lasts all summer, followed by red berries. Give the plant a warm, sheltered spot and some winter protection; alternatively, grow it in a conservatory. Grow in fertile, humus-rich, moist, but well-drained soil.

12ft / 12ft

⤡ height and spread   ✳ feature of interest   ▭ season of interest   *CLIMBERS I – L*

CLIMBERS

LONICERA X HECKROTTII ❷ 6–9
HONEYSUCKLE
CAPRIFOLIACEAE

A slow-growing honeysuckle, this is one of the best for combining with other climbers, such as a purple-flowered clematis. Best grown against wire supports. The scented flowers are pink with yellow, and are followed by red berries. Grow in fertile, humus-rich, moist, but well-drained soil.

LONICERA HENRYI ❷ 5–9
HONEYSUCKLE
CAPRIFOLIACEAE

This is a vigorous, semievergreen (or sometimes evergreen) honeysuckle with good foliage cover. Perfect for covering a large wall or fence. The purple-red flowers are small, but the display of grapelike, purple-black berries in autumn is an unusual feature. Grow in fertile, humus-rich, moist, well-drained soil.

LONICERA X ITALICA ❷ 5–11
HONEYSUCKLE
CAPRIFOLIACEAE

This is a late-flowering honeysuckle, blooming from midsummer through to the autumn. The scented flowers are yellow suffused with pink and purple, giving the impression from a distance of a pinkish-red. Like all climbing honeysuckles it twines, but there are often a few wayward shoots that need tying in.

LONICERA JAPONICA 'AUREORETICULATA' ❷ 4–10
JAPANESE HONEYSUCKLE
CAPRIFOLIACEAE

This variegated form is worth growing in a container so that it can be brought under cover in winter. The small leaves have a network of yellow veins. For the best display of flowers, choose a site that is warm and sheltered, but watch out for mildew. Grow in fertile, humus-rich, moist, but well-drained soil.

LONICERA JAPONICA 'HALLIANA' ❷ 5–10
JAPANESE HONEYSUCKLE
CAPRIFOLIACEAE

A very fragrant honeysuckle, this is perfect for quickly covering up eyesores or growing up arches or arbors. The main flower display appears in summer, and the flowers open white then age to yellow. Small black berries follow flowering. Grow in fertile, humus-rich, moist, but well-drained soil.

LONICERA PERICLYMENUM 'SEROTINA' ❷ 5–9
LATE DUTCH HONEYSUCKLE
CAPRIFOLIACEAE

A late-flowering variety with bronze-purple flushed leaves and maroon and cream flowers from midsummer to autumn. The fragrant flowers are followed by purple-red berries. In a small garden it could be grown in a container or trained as a standard. Grow in fertile, humus-rich, moist, but well-drained soil.

≣ leaf type   ● light preference   ♨ speed of growth   ✿ ease of growth

LONICERA X TELLMANNIANA Ⓩ 7–9
CAPRIFOLIACEAE

A noteworthy hybrid honeysuckle, this is grown for its large flowers and lush foliage. The golden yellow, almost copper-tinted flowers are borne in generous clusters, but unfortunately there is no scent. It is suitable for brightening up a shady wall in early summer. Grow in fertile, humus-rich, moist, well-drained soil.

LONICERA TRAGOPHYLLA Ⓩ 6–9
HONEYSUCKLE
CAPRIFOLIACEAE

A honeysuckle bearing large, bright yellow flowers that will thrive in a cool, lightly shady site. The flowers have no scent, but red berries follow flowering. The leaves are flushed with purple. Grow in fertile, humus-rich, moist, but well-drained soil.

LOPHOSPERMUM ERUBESCENS Ⓩ 9–10
CREEPING GLOXINIA
SCROPHULARIACEAE

A Mexican climber with gloxinia-type flowers. In summer rose-pink trumpet flowers hang down among the gray-green, triangular leaves. An evergreen perennial grown as a half-hardy annual, it needs a sunny position in a soil that is moist, but well drained and humus-rich.

MUTISIA OLIGODON Ⓩ 9–10
ASTERACEAE

Mutisia is a South American genus of daisy-flowered climbers, most of which are tender. This pink-flowered species is reasonably hardy, however. It needs fertile soil in a warm position, with some shade at the base and the top of the plant in the sun. The ideal place would be up a climber that has gone bare at the base.

PARTHENOCISSUS HENRYANA Ⓩ 7–8
CHINESE CREEPER
VITACEAE

This is a very vigorous plant that has beautiful, hand-shaped foliage. The leaves are dark green with silver-white veining, and they become increasingly red over summer, culminating in vivid orange in autumn. Let it romp up an evergreen tree or cover a large, cold wall. Likes fertile, well-drained soil.

PARTHENOCISSUS QUINQUEFOLIA Ⓩ 3–9
VIRGINIA CREEPER
VITACEAE

One of a family of 10 species found in forests in North America, Asia, and the Himalayas, this variety has palmate, plain leaves that come alive in autumn, when they turn brilliant red. Needs fertile, well-drained soil, and young plants are best supported.

---

 height and spread   ✳ feature of interest   ▮▮▮▮ season of interest   *CLIMBERS* **L – P**

CLIMBERS

PARTHENOCISSUS TRICUSPIDATA 'VEITCHII' **Z** 4–8
BOSTON IVY
VITACEAE

A fast-growing but densely foliaged climber for large walls. One plant can turn a 33–39ft (10–12m) length of railing or chain-link fence into a living hedge. The small, 3-lobed leaves are mid-green in spring, turn darker in summer and finally become vivid crimson and purple by autumn. Likes most soils.

PASSIFLORA CAERULEA **Z** 7–9
BLUE PASSION FLOWER
PASSIFLORACEAE

Passion flowers are grown for their fascinating fragrant flowers, which open only on sunny days. Sometimes egglike orange fruits appear. Hardy in mild areas, this is worth trying against a sunny, sheltered wall or tall fence; otherwise, grow in a pot. Requires moderately fertile, moist, but well-drained soil.

PERIPLOCA GRAECA **Z** 7–9
SILK VINE
ASCLEPIADACEAE

A twining climber indigenous to Southern Europe and parts of Asia. Has glossy, dark green leaves and, in summer, star-shaped greenish-yellow flowers which carry an unpleasant odor. Good against a wall, or over a pergola. Likes most soils. Poisonous sap.

PHASEOLUS COCCINEUS **Z** 4–11
CORKSCREW FLOWER, SNAIL BEAN
LEGUMINOSAE

These annual climbers need shelter and support—usually a wigwam or a double row of bamboo canes put in place before planting out after the last frosts have passed. As well as plentiful crops of runner beans, the attractive flowers make an effective quick screen. Grow in fertile, moist, but well-drained soil.

PILEOSTEGIA VIBURNOIDES **Z** 7–10
PILEOSTEGIA
HYDRANGEACEAE

This evergreen climbing plant, formerly known as *Schizophragma viburnoides*, is tolerant of most conditions, although it dislikes cold winds. The long, oblong leaves are an attractive feature, combined with the clusters of small, creamy white flowers. A good slow-growing plant for a shaded wall.

RHODOCHITON ATROSANGUINEUS **Z** 9–11
PURPLE BELL VINE
SCROPHULARIACEAE

A profusion of unusual flowers dangle among the heart-shaped foliage. A versatile container subject, it can either be allowed to cascade down a tall planter or trained up a lightweight tripod or trellis. Another option is to train it up a shrub. Easily raised as a half-hardy annual. Grow in fertile, humus-rich, well-drained soil.

 leaf type   light preference   speed of growth   ease of growth

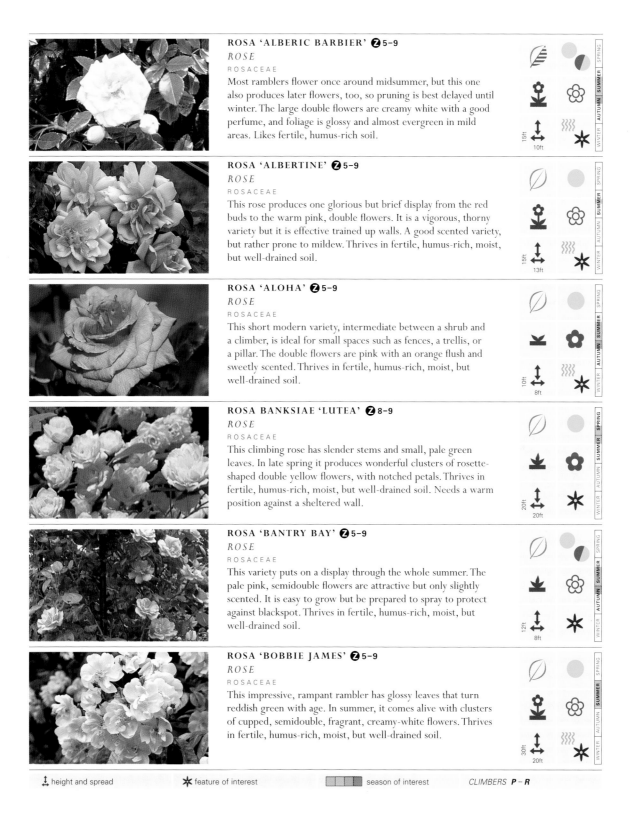

ROSA 'ALBERIC BARBIER' ❷ 5–9
ROSE

ROSACEAE

Most ramblers flower once around midsummer, but this one also produces later flowers, too, so pruning is best delayed until winter. The large double flowers are creamy white with a good perfume, and foliage is glossy and almost evergreen in mild areas. Likes fertile, humus-rich soil.

15ft / 10ft

ROSA 'ALBERTINE' ❷ 5–9
ROSE

ROSACEAE

This rose produces one glorious but brief display from the red buds to the warm pink, double flowers. It is a vigorous, thorny variety but it is effective trained up walls. A good scented variety, but rather prone to mildew. Thrives in fertile, humus-rich, moist, but well-drained soil.

15ft / 13ft

ROSA 'ALOHA' ❷ 5–9
ROSE

ROSACEAE

This short modern variety, intermediate between a shrub and a climber, is ideal for small spaces such as fences, a trellis, or a pillar. The double flowers are pink with an orange flush and sweetly scented. Thrives in fertile, humus-rich, moist, but well-drained soil.

10ft / 8ft

ROSA BANKSIAE 'LUTEA' ❷ 8–9
ROSE

ROSACEAE

This climbing rose has slender stems and small, pale green leaves. In late spring it produces wonderful clusters of rosette-shaped double yellow flowers, with notched petals. Thrives in fertile, humus-rich, moist, but well-drained soil. Needs a warm position against a sheltered wall.

20ft / 20ft

ROSA 'BANTRY BAY' ❷ 5–9
ROSE

ROSACEAE

This variety puts on a display through the whole summer. The pale pink, semidouble flowers are attractive but only slightly scented. It is easy to grow but be prepared to spray to protect against blackspot. Thrives in fertile, humus-rich, moist, but well-drained soil.

12ft / 8ft

ROSA 'BOBBIE JAMES' ❷ 5–9
ROSE

ROSACEAE

This impressive, rampant rambler has glossy leaves that turn reddish green with age. In summer, it comes alive with clusters of cupped, semidouble, fragrant, creamy-white flowers. Thrives in fertile, humus-rich, moist, but well-drained soil.

30ft / 20ft

⬍ height and spread   ✳ feature of interest   ▮▮▮▮ season of interest   *CLIMBERS* **P – R**

CLIMBERS

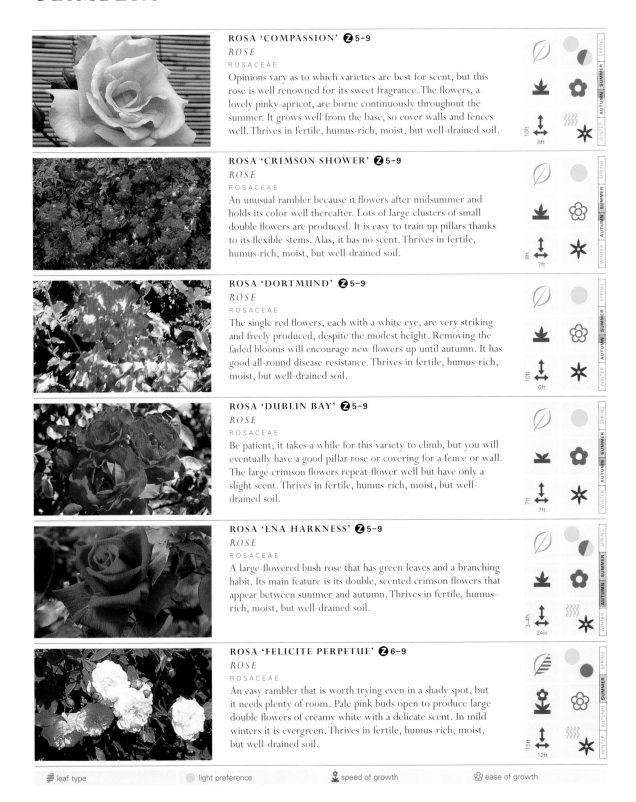

ROSA 'COMPASSION' ⓩ 5–9
ROSE
ROSACEAE

Opinions vary as to which varieties are best for scent, but this rose is well renowned for its sweet fragrance. The flowers, a lovely pinky-apricot, are borne continuously throughout the summer. It grows well from the base, so cover walls and fences well. Thrives in fertile, humus-rich, moist, but well-drained soil.

10ft 8ft

ROSA 'CRIMSON SHOWER' ⓩ 5–9
ROSE
ROSACEAE

An unusual rambler because it flowers after midsummer and holds its color well thereafter. Lots of large clusters of small double flowers are produced. It is easy to train up pillars thanks to its flexible stems. Alas, it has no scent. Thrives in fertile, humus-rich, moist, but well-drained soil.

8ft 7ft

ROSA 'DORTMUND' ⓩ 5–9
ROSE
ROSACEAE

The single red flowers, each with a white eye, are very striking and freely produced, despite the modest height. Removing the faded blooms will encourage new flowers up until autumn. It has good all-round disease resistance. Thrives in fertile, humus-rich, moist, but well-drained soil.

10ft 6ft

ROSA 'DUBLIN BAY' ⓩ 5–9
ROSE
ROSACEAE

Be patient; it takes a while for this variety to climb, but you will eventually have a good pillar rose or covering for a fence or wall. The large crimson flowers repeat-flower well but have only a slight scent. Thrives in fertile, humus-rich, moist, but well-drained soil.

7ft 7ft

ROSA 'ENA HARKNESS' ⓩ 5–9
ROSE
ROSACEAE

A large-flowered bush rose that has green leaves and a branching habit. Its main feature is its double, scented crimson flowers that appear between summer and autumn. Thrives in fertile, humus-rich, moist, but well-drained soil.

3–4ft 24in

ROSA 'FELICITE PERPETUE' ⓩ 6–9
ROSE
ROSACEAE

An easy rambler that is worth trying even in a shady spot, but it needs plenty of room. Pale pink buds open to produce large double flowers of creamy white with a delicate scent. In mild winters it is evergreen. Thrives in fertile, humus-rich, moist, but well-drained soil.

15ft 12ft

≣ leaf type   ● light preference   ☙ speed of growth   ⚘ ease of growth

ROSA FILIPES 'KIFTSGATE' ❷ 6–9
ROSE
ROSACEAE

This rampant climbing rose has an abundance of glossy leaves, composed of narrowly elliptic leaflets. It sports dense clusters of single, fragrant, creamy white flowers in late summer. Thrives in fertile, humus-rich, moist, but well-drained soil.

30ft / 20ft

ROSA 'FRANÇOIS JURANVILLE' ❷ 5–9
ROSE
ROSACEAE

Flexible stems make this variety easy to train up arches and pillars. The large, double, salmon-pink flowers have a sweet scent. The foliage is bronze when young then dark green, and makes a good foil for the warm-colored blooms. Thrives in fertile, humus-rich, moist, but well-drained soil.

20ft / 15ft

ROSA 'GOLDEN SHOWERS' ❷ 5–9
ROSE
ROSACEAE

This is a modern climber that provides plenty of flowers. The double, bright yellow blooms fade to a paler yellow with age. The stems are long and thornless, making it good for training or for cut flowers. It has good all-round disease resistance. Thrives in fertile, humus-rich, moist, but well-drained soil.

10ft / 6ft

ROSA 'GOLDFINCH' ❷ 5–9
ROSE
ROSACEAE

This small-flowered rambler has bright green foliage. Each bloom is semidouble and a creamy yellow, with a fruity scent, and tends to fade to white in the sun. It is a fairly short variety but quite bushy and almost thornless. Thrives in fertile, humus-rich, moist, but well-drained soil.

8ft / 6ft

ROSA 'HANDEL' ❷ 5–9
ROSE
ROSACEAE

The bright flowers need careful placing in the garden, but its vigor makes this variety a good choice for covering a wall. The double blooms are cream with bright rose-red edges. It flowers well into autumn, but there is only a slight scent. Thrives in fertile, humus-rich, moist, but well-drained soil.

10ft / 7ft

ROSA 'LAURA FORD' ❷ 5–9
ROSE
ROSACEAE

One of the new miniature climbers, this variety is perfect for covering an obelisk. The mini flowers and leaves would be ideal in a container but it must be kept watered and fed regularly. The double yellow flowers develop a pink flush in direct sun. Likes fertile, humus-rich, moist, but well-drained soil.

7ft / 4ft

⟂ height and spread   ✳ feature of interest   ▮▮▮▮ season of interest   *CLIMBERS* **R**

CLIMBERS

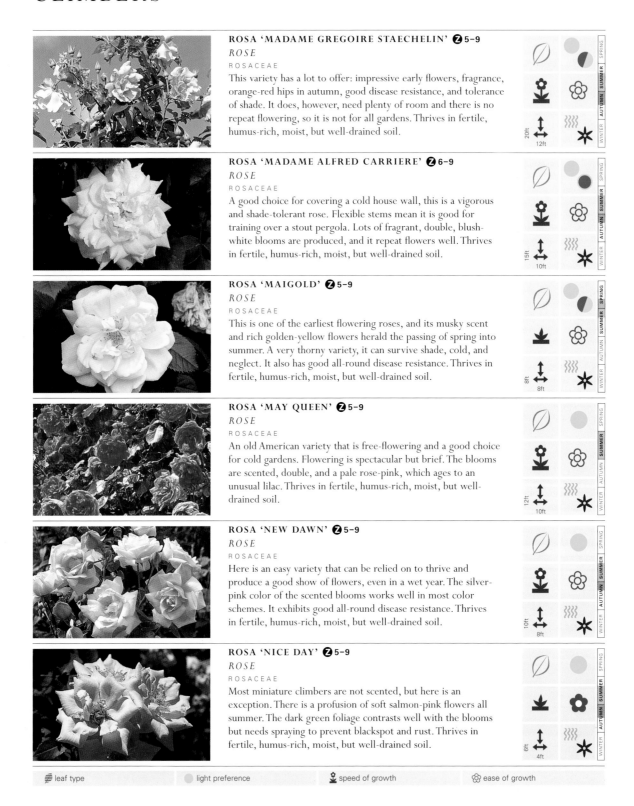

ROSA 'MADAME GREGOIRE STAECHELIN' ❷ 5–9
ROSE
ROSACEAE

This variety has a lot to offer: impressive early flowers, fragrance, orange-red hips in autumn, good disease resistance, and tolerance of shade. It does, however, need plenty of room and there is no repeat flowering, so it is not for all gardens. Thrives in fertile, humus-rich, moist, but well-drained soil.

ROSA 'MADAME ALFRED CARRIERE' ❷ 6–9
ROSE
ROSACEAE

A good choice for covering a cold house wall, this is a vigorous and shade-tolerant rose. Flexible stems mean it is good for training over a stout pergola. Lots of fragrant, double, blush-white blooms are produced, and it repeat flowers well. Thrives in fertile, humus-rich, moist, but well-drained soil.

ROSA 'MAIGOLD' ❷ 5–9
ROSE
ROSACEAE

This is one of the earliest flowering roses, and its musky scent and rich golden-yellow flowers herald the passing of spring into summer. A very thorny variety, it can survive shade, cold, and neglect. It also has good all-round disease resistance. Thrives in fertile, humus-rich, moist, but well-drained soil.

ROSA 'MAY QUEEN' ❷ 5–9
ROSE
ROSACEAE

An old American variety that is free-flowering and a good choice for cold gardens. Flowering is spectacular but brief. The blooms are scented, double, and a pale rose-pink, which ages to an unusual lilac. Thrives in fertile, humus-rich, moist, but well-drained soil.

ROSA 'NEW DAWN' ❷ 5–9
ROSE
ROSACEAE

Here is an easy variety that can be relied on to thrive and produce a good show of flowers, even in a wet year. The silver-pink color of the scented blooms works well in most color schemes. It exhibits good all-round disease resistance. Thrives in fertile, humus-rich, moist, but well-drained soil.

ROSA 'NICE DAY' ❷ 5–9
ROSE
ROSACEAE

Most miniature climbers are not scented, but here is an exception. There is a profusion of soft salmon-pink flowers all summer. The dark green foliage contrasts well with the blooms but needs spraying to prevent blackspot and rust. Thrives in fertile, humus-rich, moist, but well-drained soil.

🍃 leaf type   ● light preference   🌱 speed of growth   🕸 ease of growth

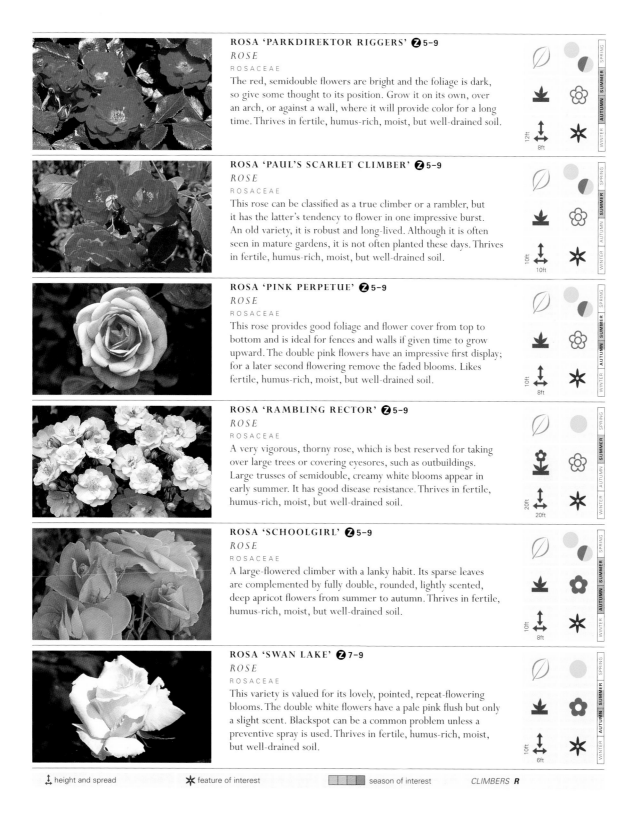

ROSA 'PARKDIREKTOR RIGGERS' ⓩ5–9
ROSE
ROSACEAE

The red, semidouble flowers are bright and the foliage is dark, so give some thought to its position. Grow it on its own, over an arch, or against a wall, where it will provide color for a long time. Thrives in fertile, humus-rich, moist, but well-drained soil.

ROSA 'PAUL'S SCARLET CLIMBER' ⓩ5–9
ROSE
ROSACEAE

This rose can be classified as a true climber or a rambler, but it has the latter's tendency to flower in one impressive burst. An old variety, it is robust and long-lived. Although it is often seen in mature gardens, it is not often planted these days. Thrives in fertile, humus-rich, moist, but well-drained soil.

ROSA 'PINK PERPETUE' ⓩ5–9
ROSE
ROSACEAE

This rose provides good foliage and flower cover from top to bottom and is ideal for fences and walls if given time to grow upward. The double pink flowers have an impressive first display; for a later second flowering remove the faded blooms. Likes fertile, humus-rich, moist, but well-drained soil.

ROSA 'RAMBLING RECTOR' ⓩ5–9
ROSE
ROSACEAE

A very vigorous, thorny rose, which is best reserved for taking over large trees or covering eyesores, such as outbuildings. Large trusses of semidouble, creamy white blooms appear in early summer. It has good disease resistance. Thrives in fertile, humus-rich, moist, but well-drained soil.

ROSA 'SCHOOLGIRL' ⓩ5–9
ROSE
ROSACEAE

A large-flowered climber with a lanky habit. Its sparse leaves are complemented by fully double, rounded, lightly scented, deep apricot flowers from summer to autumn. Thrives in fertile, humus-rich, moist, but well-drained soil.

ROSA 'SWAN LAKE' ⓩ7–9
ROSE
ROSACEAE

This variety is valued for its lovely, pointed, repeat-flowering blooms. The double white flowers have a pale pink flush but only a slight scent. Blackspot can be a common problem unless a preventive spray is used. Thrives in fertile, humus-rich, moist, but well-drained soil.

↥ height and spread   ✹ feature of interest   ▢▢▢ season of interest   *CLIMBERS* **R**

CLIMBERS

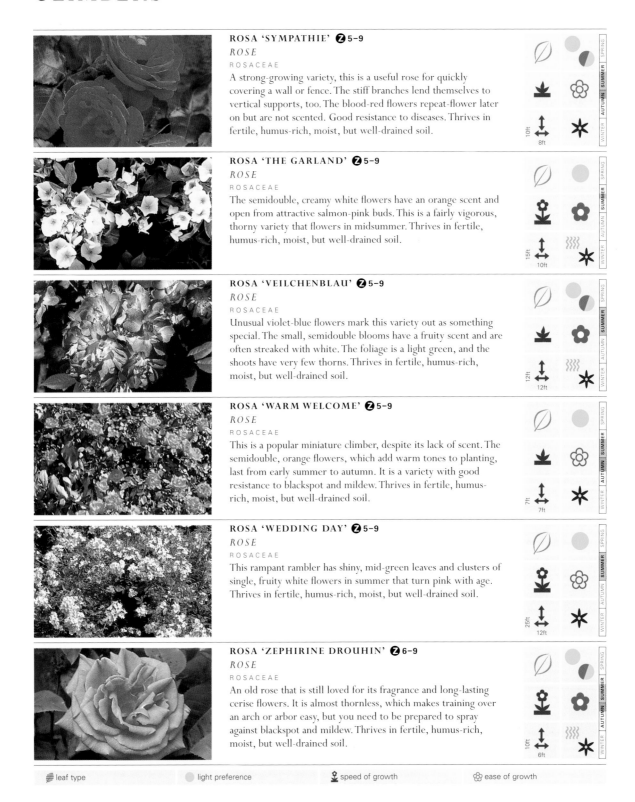

ROSA 'SYMPATHIE' ❷ 5–9
ROSE
ROSACEAE
A strong-growing variety, this is a useful rose for quickly covering a wall or fence. The stiff branches lend themselves to vertical supports, too. The blood-red flowers repeat-flower later on but are not scented. Good resistance to diseases. Thrives in fertile, humus-rich, moist, but well-drained soil.

10ft / 8ft

ROSA 'THE GARLAND' ❷ 5–9
ROSE
ROSACEAE
The semidouble, creamy white flowers have an orange scent and open from attractive salmon-pink buds. This is a fairly vigorous, thorny variety that flowers in midsummer. Thrives in fertile, humus-rich, moist, but well-drained soil.

15ft / 10ft

ROSA 'VEILCHENBLAU' ❷ 5–9
ROSE
ROSACEAE
Unusual violet-blue flowers mark this variety out as something special. The small, semidouble blooms have a fruity scent and are often streaked with white. The foliage is a light green, and the shoots have very few thorns. Thrives in fertile, humus-rich, moist, but well-drained soil.

12ft / 12ft

ROSA 'WARM WELCOME' ❷ 5–9
ROSE
ROSACEAE
This is a popular miniature climber, despite its lack of scent. The semidouble, orange flowers, which add warm tones to planting, last from early summer to autumn. It is a variety with good resistance to blackspot and mildew. Thrives in fertile, humus-rich, moist, but well-drained soil.

7ft / 7ft

ROSA 'WEDDING DAY' ❷ 5–9
ROSE
ROSACEAE
This rampant rambler has shiny, mid-green leaves and clusters of single, fruity white flowers in summer that turn pink with age. Thrives in fertile, humus-rich, moist, but well-drained soil.

25ft / 12ft

ROSA 'ZEPHIRINE DROUHIN' ❷ 6–9
ROSE
ROSACEAE
An old rose that is still loved for its fragrance and long-lasting cerise flowers. It is almost thornless, which makes training over an arch or arbor easy, but you need to be prepared to spray against blackspot and mildew. Thrives in fertile, humus-rich, moist, but well-drained soil.

10ft / 6ft

🌿 leaf type   ● light preference   ♟ speed of growth   ✿ ease of growth

SCHISANDRA RUBRIFLORA ❷ 7–9

SCHISANDRACEAE

Indigenous to parts of India, West China, and Burma, this woody climber has elegant red shoots and lance-shaped, toothed green leaves. From late spring to summer, it produces single, dark red flowers, and female plants follow up by bearing spikes of fleshy red fruit. Needs fertile, moist, but well-drained soil to do well.

SCHIZOPHRAGMA HYDRANGEOIDES ❷ 6–9

HYDRANGEACEAE

Originally found on cliffs and woodland in Japan and other parts of Asia, this woody climber has small, fragrant white flowers in terminal cymes in midsummer. Requires fertile, humus-rich, moist, but well-drained soil and benefits from being grown against a wall, fence, or other type of boundary.

SCHIZOPHRAGMA INTEGRIFOLIUM ❷ 5–9

HYDRANGEACEAE

A relative of the climbing hydrangea, this is more impressive although it takes longer to mature. It has broad, oval-shaped leaves and particularly large, hydrangealike flowers. Ideal for scaling a large tree or house wall, it must be tied to supports until the aerial roots take hold. Requires fertile, humus-rich, moist, but well-drained soil.

SENECIO SCANDENS ❷ 9–10

ASTERACEAE

This is an evergreen perennial with long trailing stems. Treat it as a climber in mild areas or as a conservatory plant in cold gardens. The yellow daisy flowers are not dramatic but are in keeping with natural or wildflower gardens. Allow it to tumble over hedges and low fences to suit its semiwild appearance. Grow in moist, gritty soil.

SOLANUM DULCAMARA 'VARIEGATUM' ❷ 5–9

VARIEGATED NIGHTSHADE

SOLANACEAE

This is a perennial climber that dies back each autumn. It has attractive cream-splashed leaves which makes it worth growing. The flowers are small and violet. Their shape is typical of the nightshade family. The black fruit are attractive but poisonous. A plant where low climbers are required. A vicious weed.

SOLANUM JASMINOIDES ❷ 8–10

POTATO VINE

SOLANACEAE

This scrambling climber has attractive, slim, lance-shaped leaves, and in summer and autumn it will carry fragrant, blue-white flowers with yellow anthers. These are followed by little black fruit. Needs moderately fertile, moist, but well-drained soil—slightly alkaline if possible.

---

 height and spread　　　 feature of interest　　　 season of interest　　　*CLIMBERS* **R – S**

CLIMBERS

THUNBERGIA ALATA Z 10–11

BLACK-EYED SUSAN

ACANTHACEAE

An easy plant bearing orange, yellow, or white flowers, often with brown-purple centers. A perennial that is grown as a half-hardy annual, use it to brighten up a fence or as a patio plant. In a container growth will be no more than 3ft (1m); train it up a tripod or allow it to trail. Grow in moist, well-drained soil.

8ft / 12in

TRACHELOSPERMUM ASIATICUM Z 9–10

APOCYNACEAE

This jasmine has both good flower and foliage features. The small, white, starlike flowers release a sweet scent. The evergreen foliage consists of leathery, dark green, lance-shaped leaves, some of which turn red in winter. Although slightly hardier than the star jasmine (see below), it is still best grown against a warm wall. Grow in fertile, well-drained soil.

20ft / 20ft

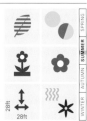

TRACHELOSPERMUM JASMINOIDES Z 9–10

STAR JASMINE

APOCYNACEAE

This is similar in appearance to *T. asiaticum*, but the flowers are more fragrant. Although vigorous, it is not reliably hardy and may need to be grown in a container and moved under glass in cold gardens. In milder gardens it makes an impressive climber for an arbor or pergola. Grow in fertile, well-drained soil.

28ft / 28ft

TROPAEOLUM MAJUS Z 8–11

CLIMBING NASTURTIUM

TROPAEOLACEAE

These annuals offer a quick solution to a patch of dry, poor soil or an eyesore. Climbing varieties can be allowed to scramble over fences or can be trained up string or canes. These are easy annuals, although prone to insects. Grow in moderately fertile, moist, but well-drained soil.

3–10ft / 5–15ft

TROPAEOLUM PEREGRINUM Z 9–10

CANARY CREEPER

TROPAEOLACEAE

Originally from mountainous areas of Ecuador and Peru, this strong herbaceous climber has light to grayish-green leaves and produces hooked, yellow flowers from summer to autumn. Great for hanging baskets or for trailing down or growing up a wall. Requires moist, but well-drained, fertile soil.

8–12ft / 8–12ft

TROPAEOLUM SPECIOSUM Z 8–10

SCOTTISH FLAME FLOWER, FLAME CREEPER

TROPAEOLACEAE

Flamboyant flame flowers, then bright blue berries are the features of this Chilean perennial nasturtium. Very effective when grown over shrubs or up a dark evergreen hedge, it climbs by coiling leaf stalks. It needs a cool, moist soil.

10ft / 10ft

leaf type | light preference | speed of growth | ease of growth

TROPAEOLUM TUBEROSUM ⓩ8–10
PERUVIAN FLAME FLOWER
TROPAEOLACEAE

A perennial with vibrant orange-red flowers, this grows from edible tubers each year. Although the tubers often survive in mild winters, they are best dug up and overwintered in cold gardens. It climbs by means of coiling leaf stalks. Grow in moist, but well-drained soil.

6–12ft / 6–12ft

VITIS COIGNETIAE ⓩ5–9
CRIMSON GLORY VINE
VITACEAE

This is the most spectacular vine for foliage if you have a large wall, outbuilding, or mature tree. It reaches 11ft (3.5m) in five years but is a long-lived plant. Use it as an impressive backdrop. It does best in poor soil, and the grapes are inedible. Vines need to be attached to supports by wires.

30ft / 30ft

VITIS VINIFERA 'PURPUREA' ⓩ6–9
PURPLE-LEAVED VINE
VITACEAE

This variety is a woody climber with rounded, 3- to 5-lobed toothed leaves which start out gray and hairy and progress to plum-colored before becoming dark purple in autumn. Grow in well-drained, fertile soil.

22ft / 22ft

WISTERIA BRACHYBOTRYS 'SHIRO-KABITAN' ⓩ6–9
PAPILIONACEAE

This an unusual form of wisteria in that the racemes of flowers are much shorter and broader than in the more common forms. It has long been grown in Japan where it is appreciated for its glisteningly white flowers and its velvety leaves which, when young, have a silvery sheen. It is twining like the other forms of wisteria, but it is not so rampant.

28ft / 28ft

WISTERIA FLORIBUNDA 'MACROBOTRYS' ⓩ5–9
JAPANESE WISTERIA
PAPILIONACEAE

The most spectacular of all wisteria, the racemes of dark purple flowers far exceed any other variety in length. Grow on a stout pergola fitted with strong wires, then you can see the flowers hanging freely. Brief flowering is followed by seed pods and yellow autumn foliage. Likes fertile, well-drained soil.

30ft / 30ft

WISTERIA SINENSIS ⓩ5–8
CHINESE WISTERIA
PAPILIONACEAE

This species grows more quickly than *W. floribunda*. In addition to the species, several named varieties are grown, and these are the best wisteria for wall-training, flowering slightly earlier than *W. floribunda*. Wisteria take nearly five years to flower; avoid seed-raised plants, which can take fifteen years or more.

30ft / 30ft

⬍ height and spread   ✳ feature of interest   ▭▭▭ season of interest   *CLIMBERS* **T – W**

TREES AND CONIFERS

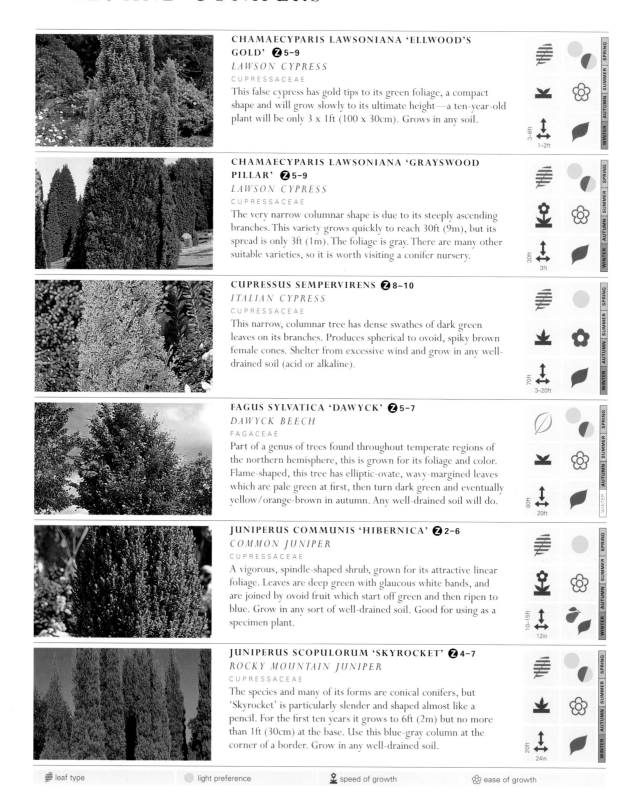

CHAMAECYPARIS LAWSONIANA 'ELLWOOD'S GOLD' **Z** 5–9
LAWSON CYPRESS
CUPRESSACEAE

This false cypress has gold tips to its green foliage, a compact shape and will grow slowly to its ultimate height—a ten-year-old plant will be only 3 x 1ft (100 x 30cm). Grows in any soil.

CHAMAECYPARIS LAWSONIANA 'GRAYSWOOD PILLAR' **Z** 5–9
LAWSON CYPRESS
CUPRESSACEAE

The very narrow columnar shape is due to its steeply ascending branches. This variety grows quickly to reach 30ft (9m), but its spread is only 3ft (1m). The foliage is gray. There are many other suitable varieties, so it is worth visiting a conifer nursery.

CUPRESSUS SEMPERVIRENS **Z** 8–10
ITALIAN CYPRESS
CUPRESSACEAE

This narrow, columnar tree has dense swathes of dark green leaves on its branches. Produces spherical to ovoid, spiky brown female cones. Shelter from excessive wind and grow in any well-drained soil (acid or alkaline).

FAGUS SYLVATICA 'DAWYCK' **Z** 5–7
DAWYCK BEECH
FAGACEAE

Part of a genus of trees found throughout temperate regions of the northern hemisphere, this is grown for its foliage and color. Flame-shaped, this tree has elliptic-ovate, wavy-margined leaves which are pale green at first, then turn dark green and eventually yellow/orange-brown in autumn. Any well-drained soil will do.

JUNIPERUS COMMUNIS 'HIBERNICA' **Z** 2–6
COMMON JUNIPER
CUPRESSACEAE

A vigorous, spindle-shaped shrub, grown for its attractive linear foliage. Leaves are deep green with glaucous white bands, and are joined by ovoid fruit which start off green and then ripen to blue. Grow in any sort of well-drained soil. Good for using as a specimen plant.

JUNIPERUS SCOPULORUM 'SKYROCKET' **Z** 4–7
ROCKY MOUNTAIN JUNIPER
CUPRESSACEAE

The species and many of its forms are conical conifers, but 'Skyrocket' is particularly slender and shaped almost like a pencil. For the first ten years it grows to 6ft (2m) but no more than 1ft (30cm) at the base. Use this blue-gray column at the corner of a border. Grow in any well-drained soil.

leaf type   light preference   speed of growth   ease of growth

LIRIODENDRON TULIPIFERA 'FASTIGIATUM' ❷5–9
TULIP TREE
MAGNOLIACEAE

Part of a genus originally from China, North America, and Vietnam, this is a vigorous tree with large dark green leaves that yellow as autumn arrives. Pale green flowers with orange bands arrive in midsummer, followed by conelike fruits. Grow in moderately fertile, slightly acid, moist, but well-drained soil.

70ft / 25ft

MALUS 'BALLERINA HYBRIDS' ❷4–8
BALLERINA APPLE TREES
ROSACEAE

These hybrids have been bred for small gardens. Instead of being the usual apple-tree shape, they consist of a single upright stem to take up very little space. They can be used in the open ground and also in containers. Unlike other types of apple trees, these are all new varieties.

10ft / 6ft

PRUNUS 'AMANOGAWA' ❷6–8
ORNAMENTAL CHERRY
ROSACEAE

An upright tree with foliage that displays an attractive range of color throughout the seasons. Yellowish-bronze in spring, by autumn the tree can be sporting green, yellow, and red leaves at the same time. It has saucer-shaped flowers in spring which are pink and fragrant. Grow in moist, but well-drained, fertile soil.

25ft / 12ft

QUERCUS ROBUR 'FASTIGIATA' ❷5–8
FASTIGIATE OAK
FAGACEAE

This handsome cultivar has upright branches, gray-brown bark, and short-stalked, dark green leaves. Ovoid acorns can appear either singly or in clusters. This genus requires deep, fertile, well-drained soil.

50ft / 50ft

SORBUS AUCUPARIA 'FASTIGIATA' ❷4–7
ROWAN
ROSACEAE

Considering the small ground space this plant occupies, it offers a lot of seasonal features. After ten years it will be 13 x 3ft (4 x 1m). The foliage is attractively divided. In late spring there are white flowers followed by red berries and autumn tints. Grow in a well-drained, moderately fertile, humus-rich soil.

25ft / 15ft

TAXUS BACCATA 'FASTIGIATA' ❷7–8
IRISH YEW
TAXACEAE

Its slow growth and shape make this yew invaluable as a living focal point. It can be used singly, planted each side of an entrance, or in a line to form a screen. Becomes straggly and dull in heavy shade. Only female forms will bear fruit. Most parts of yew are poisonous. Grow in any well-drained, fertile soil.

30ft / 20ft

---

 height and spread   ✳ feature of interest   ▮▮▮▮ season of interest   *TREES AND CONIFERS* **C – T**

FRUIT

FICUS CARICA ❷ 6–10
FIG
MORACEAE

Figs need a warm climate to crop well, but a fan-trained plant will often produce a few figs in a warm, sheltered spot. Winter protection is needed. Restrict the roots in a pot or lined pit to limit the vigor. Figs can be grown in 18in (45cm) diameter containers, but a lot of pruning is needed. Likes fertile soils.

MALUS DOMESTICA ❷ 3–8
APPLE
ROSACEAE

Apple trees with on a dwarfing rootstock can occupy a small space if they are trained and pruned carefully. Use an espalier apple whose ladderlike arrangement of branches will look wonderful when covered in pink and white blossom in spring. Most varieties need a pollinator.

PRUNUS ARMENIACA ❷ 3–9
APRICOT
ROSACEAE

Apricots are not difficult to grow but since they flower early they are prone to losing all the blossom, and consequently the fruit, to frost unless protection can be provided. They can be grown as freestanding trees, but do best trained against warm walls. Apart from the fruit, apricot trees in blossom are very ornamental.

PRUNUS CERASUS ❷ 4–8
CHERRY
ROSACEAE

In colder regions sweet cherries are best fan-trained against a sunny wall: cropping will be better and a fan is easier to net against birds. Heights and spreads assume a Colt rootstock. Self-fertile varieties, such as *P. a.* 'Stella', do not need a pollinator. Sour cherries can be grown on a shaded wall, in any moist, well-drained soil.

PRUNUS DOMESTICA ❷ 4–10
PLUM
ROSACEAE

A dwarf plum pyramid, using a 'Pixy' rootstock, needs only light pruning, so reducing the chances of silver leaf disease. Fan-training against a warm wall or fence in cooler gardens helps provide the extra shelter and sun needed for a good crop. A pollinator may be required. Likes most soils.

PRUNUS PERSICA ❷ 4–9
PEACH
ROSACEAE

The best way to grow a peach in a cool climate is to train it as a fan against a warm, sunny wall or fence. To guard against fungal disease, such as peach leaf curl, cover in winter with clear plastic secured to a wooden frame. Most varieties are self-fertile. Grow in any moderately fertile, moist, but well-drained soil.

≣ leaf type   ● light preference   ⚇ speed of growth   ⚙ ease of growth

PRUNUS PERSICA VAR. NECTARINA ❷5–9
NECTARINE
ROSACEAE

Nectarines are smooth-skinned peaches and so the information given for peaches (page 106) applies. They are not as hardy as peaches so they should not be planted in cold areas. Train in a fan against a warm, sheltered wall. Grow in any moderately fertile, moist, but well-drained soil.

PYRUS COMMUNIS ❷4–9
PEAR
ROSACEAE

Pear trees are attractive so, even if an edible harvest is uncertain, there is always the early blossom and autumn color. Good yields need warmer and more sheltered conditions than apples. They can be grown as cordons, fans, or dwarf pyramids. A pollinator is required. Grow in any soil. Hardiness varies with variety.

RIBES GROSSULARIA ❷3–8
GOOSEBERRY
GROSSULARIACEAE

Gooseberries can be grown as an ordinary bush or they can be trained as a fans, cordons, or standards. Fans can be trained against walls, but generally gooseberries prefer an open position. There is a wide choice of varieties, some culinary (for cooking) others dessert (for eating uncooked). Hardiness varies with variety.

RIBES RUBRUM ❷3–7
RED CURRANT
GROSSULARIACEAE

Red currants are simple to grow and train. There is a host of options. A vertical cordon takes up the minimum of ground space, and a standard allows the ground beneath to be used by other plants. Fan-train against a wall or fence for extra warmth. Red currants are self-fertile. Grow in fertile, well-drained soil.

RUBUS FRUTICOSUS ❷3–10
BLACKBERRY AND HYBRID BERRIES
ROSACEAE

Left to their own devices, these plants would rampage along the ground. Training is all about keeping them off the ground and separating the new canes from the old. All are vigorous, but they can cope with some shade and neglect and are, therefore, suitable for growing along a back fence or wall. Grow in any soil.

VITIS VINIFERA ❷4–9
GRAPE
VITACEAE

The variety, supports, and training methods for grape plants should be chosen with care. The vertical solution is to train a standard vine in a 18in (45cm) pot. This will take at least five years, but makes an attractive feature. Grow in humus-rich, neutral to alkaline, well-drained soil. Hardiness varies with variety.

⤵ height and spread ✱ feature of interest ▯▯▯ season of interest *FRUIT* **F – V**

GLOSSARY

ALPINE: A plant that in its natural mountain habitat grows above the uppermost limit of trees. More colloquially, plants that are suitable for rock gardens are called alpines.

ANNUAL: A plant that grows from seed, flowers, and dies within the same year. Some half-hardy perennial plants are used as annuals; that is, they die off in the winter.

ANTHER: Pollen-bearing part of the stamen of a flower.

AQUATIC PLANT: A plant that lives totally or partly submerged in water.

BEDDING PLANTS: Plants that are set out for a temporary spring or summer display and discarded at the end of the season.

BIENNIAL: A plant raised from seed that makes its initial growth in one year and flowers during the following one, then dies.

BULB: An underground food storage organ formed of fleshy, modified leaves that enclose a dormant shoot.

CALYX: The outer and protective part of a flower. It is usually green and is very apparent in roses.

COMPOST: Vegetable waste from kitchens, as well as the soft parts of garden plants, which is encouraged to decompose and to form a material that can be dug into soil or used to create a mulch around plants.

CORM: An underground storage organ formed of a swollen stem base; for example, a gladiolus.

CULTIVAR: A shortened term for "cultivated variety" that indicates a variety raised in cultivation. Strictly speaking, most modern varieties are cultivars, but the term variety is still widely used because it is familiar to most gardeners.

CUTTING: A section of plant which is detached and encouraged to form roots and stems to provide a new independent plant. Cuttings may be taken from roots, stems, or leaves.

CYME: A flat-topped or dome-shaped flower head with the inner flowers opening first.

DEADHEADING: The removal of a faded flower head to prevent the formation of seeds and to encourage the development of further flowers.

DORMANT: When a plant is alive but is making no growth, it is called dormant. The dormant period is usually the winter.

EVERGREEN: Plants that appear to be green throughout the year and not to lose their leaves are called evergreen. In reality, however, they shed some of their leaves throughout the year, while producing others.

FRIABLE: Soil that is crumbly, light, and easily worked. It especially applies to soil being prepared as a seedbed in spring.

HALF-HARDY: A plant that can withstand fairly low temperatures, but needs protection from frost.

HALF-HARDY ANNUAL: An annual that is sown in gentle warmth in a greenhouse in spring, the seedlings being transferred to wider spacings in pots or boxes. The plants are placed in a garden or container only when all risk of frost has passed.

HARDEN OFF: To accustom plants raised under cover to cooler conditions so they can be planted outside.

HARDY: A plant that is able to survive outdoors in winter. In the case of some rock-garden plants, good drainage is essential to ensure their survival. Also refers to a plant that can withstand extremes of growth conditions.

HERB: A plant that is grown for its aromatic qualities and can often be used in cooking or medicinally.

HERBACEOUS PERENNIAL: A plant with no woody tissue that lives for several years. Herbaceous perennials may be deciduous or evergreen.

HYBRID: A cross between two different species, varieties, or genera.

LOAM: Friable topsoil.

MULCHING: Covering the soil around plants with well-decayed organic material, such as garden compost or peat.

NEUTRAL: Soil that is neither acid nor alkaline, with a pH of 7.0, is said to be neutral. Most plants grow in a pH of about 6.5.

PEAT: A naturally occurring substance formed from partly rotted organic material in water-logged soils, used as a growing medium and soil additive.

PERENNIAL: Any plant that lives for three or more years is called a perennial.

PERGOLA: An open timber structure made up of linked arches.

POLLINATOR: A tree or shrub planted for the purpose of supplying pollen to another plant to help in the formation of fruit, usually associated with fruit trees, many of which are not self-pollinating.

POTTING SOIL: Traditionally, a soil formed of loam, sharp sand and peat, fertilizers, and lime. The ratio of the ingredients is altered according to whether the soil is used for sowing seeds, potting-up, or repotting plants into larger containers. Recognition of the environmental importance of conserving peat beds has led to many modern soils being formed of other organic materials, such as coir or shredded bark.

PRICKING OFF: Transplanting seedlings from the container in which they were sown to one where they are more widely spaced.

RACEME: An elongated flower head with each flower having a stem.

RAISED BED: A raised area, usually encircled by a drystone wall. Rock-garden plants can be grown both in the raised bed and the wall.

RHIZOME: An underground or partly buried horizontal stem. It can be slender or fleshy. Some irises have thick, fleshy rhizomes, while those of lily-of-the-valley are slender and creeping. They act as storage organs and perpetuate plants from one season to another.

ROOTSTOCK: Plant used to provide a rooted stem onto which another plant is grafted or budded.

SEED LEAVES: The first leaves that develop on a seedling, which are coarser and more robust than the true leaves.

SEMIEVERGREEN: A plant that may keep some of its leaves in a reasonably mild winter.

SPECIES ROSE: A term for a wild rose or one of its near relatives.

SPECIMEN PLANT: A plant that is attractive enough to be grown on its own rather than in a bed or border with other plants.

STAMEN: The male part of a flower.

STANDARD: A tree or shrub trained to form a rounded head of branches at the top of a clear stem.

SUBSHRUB: Small and spreading shrub with a woody base. It differs from normal shrubs in that, in temperate regions, its upper stems and shoots die back during winter.

TENDER: A plant that will not tolerate cold conditions.

TILTH: Friable topsoil in which seeds are sown. It also acts as a mulch on the surface of soil, helping to reduce the loss of moisture from the soil's surface.

TOPSOIL: The uppermost fertile layer of soil that is suitable for plant growth.

TROUGH GARDENS: Old stone troughs partly filled with drainage material and then with freely draining soil. They are planted with miniature conifers and bulbs, as well as small rock-garden plants.

TUBER: A swollen, thickened, and fleshy stem or root. Some tubers are swollen roots (dahlia), while others are swollen stems (potato). They serve as storage organs and help to perpetuate plants from one season to another.

VARIEGATED: Usually applied to leaves and used to describe a state of having two or more colours.

VARIETY: A naturally occurring variation of a species that retains its characteristics when propagated. The term is often used for cultivars.

INDEX

HARDINESS ZONES MAP

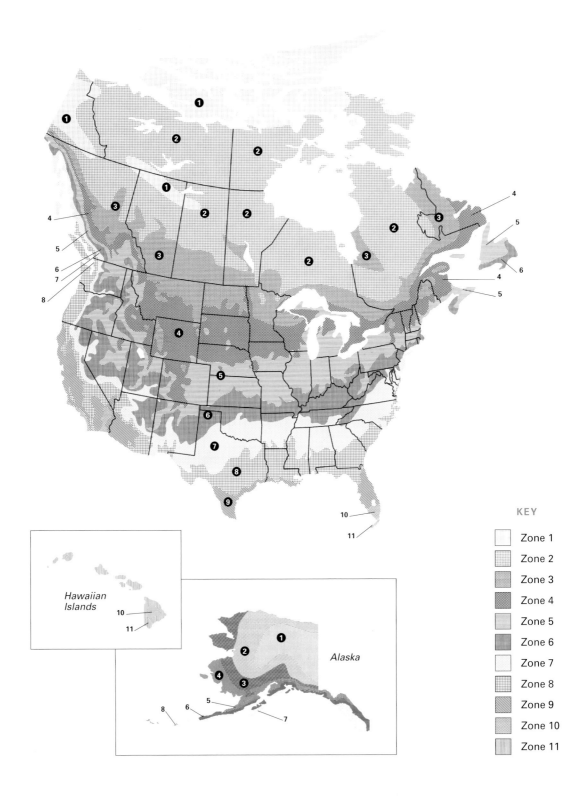

KEY

Zone 1
Zone 2
Zone 3
Zone 4
Zone 5
Zone 6
Zone 7
Zone 8
Zone 9
Zone 10
Zone 11

Hawaiian
Islands

Alaska